21: PERSPECTIVES IN CRITICISM

PERSPECTIVES IN CRITICISM

21:

Gerald Nelson

Changes of Heart:
A Study of the Poetry of W. H. Auden

UNIVERSITY OF CALIFORNIA PRESS
Berkeley and Los Angeles
1969

Grateful acknowledgment is extended to Random House, Inc., for
use of the poetry from copyrighted volumes of W. H. Auden's poems.
Please note that "Petition" and "September 1, 1939" do not appear
in the recently published COLLECTED SHORTER POEMS 1927–
1957, by W. H. Auden, by preference of Mr. Auden.

SBN: 520-01599-1
LIBRARY OF CONGRESS CATALOG CARD NO. 69-16509
Printed in the United States of America

To my parents and to Alix

Acknowledgments

I am indebted to the following individuals for both their criticism and their encouragement: George Stade and Chester Anderson of Columbia University; John Thompson and Herbert Weisinger of the State University of New York at Stony Brook; Donald Torchiana of Northwestern University; Paul Jackson of Whitman College; Frank Morral of Carleton College; David Bathrick, Chicago; and Mrs. Shirley Halperin, New York.

I am particularly grateful to my editor, Clarence Creasy; to my copy editor, Mrs. Lynda Bridge; and to John Unterecker of Columbia University for spending years rather than hours teaching me how to write.

The author is also grateful to Mr. Auden for permission to reprint the two poems "September 1, 1939" and "Petition," which Mr. Auden has decided not to include in any anthologies or collections of his works that may be published in the future.

Preface

w. h. auden no longer provokes the polemics which he inspired in the 1940s and 1950s when he was considered fair and important game by the critics who felt that he had failed to fulfill his literary promise and commitments. Although F. R. Leavis and others writing in *Scrutiny* must be given credit for beginning anti-Auden criticism and maintaining it through the years, the most influential of Auden's "angry" critics were two Americans: Randall Jarrell and Joseph Warren Beach. Jarrell felt that Auden had betrayed the liberal fight of the thirties by seeking refuge in a reconversion to Christianity, and that Auden's stand had been considerably weakened in shifting from a position of hating evil to one of accepting his own share in it; from hating Hitler to saying, "We are *all* Hitler." The result seemed to indicate to Jarrell that Auden had lost his sense of authority; that he did not know where or who he was. Beach, picking up where Jarrell left off, attacked Auden for his capriciousness in the selection and ordering of poems in *The Collected Poetry of W. H. Auden,* arguing that Auden's refusal to respect their proper chronology showed the man to be without development as a poet and the success of any individual poem to be pure accident.

Both men shared a hearty disdain for Auden's long poems of the forties, finding them diffuse in thought and uncertain in technique. Of course they are, and in a sense they have to be since Auden was trying during that period to adjust his art to his new metaphysical point of view. He was attempting to rebuild his images upon a new metaphoric base. Most importantly, he was searching for a new poetic voice, for a new persona to use in his poetry. Inasmuch as we are now familiar with Auden's later volumes, particularly *The Shield of Achilles*, Jarrell's and Beach's judgments seem superficial and misdirected, for in spite of the apparent confusion of the long poems of the forties there *is* evidence of development and direction in Auden's work. We may disagree with the motive behind the change in direction and dislike its results, but we must admit that it exists.

In order to trace this change, I shall focus directly on the poems themselves. In the case of the longer, dramatic works, this will entail examinations of the attitudes and ideas of the various characters, and in the shorter, nondramatic poems, an attempt to see the exact nature of the persona in use.

By the term persona I mean the human image within the poem, the face the reader sees behind the voice, the man one imagines to be delivering the lines. A persona is, of course, a mask a poet uses to make certain ideas or positions believable to the reader, to humanize and yet objectify states of mind and feeling. It serves, or should serve, as a meeting point between poet and reader. In dramatic poems the characters take the place of a persona, representing variations of the stand taken by the poet. In nondramatic poems, the persona must be sufficiently removed from the poet himself so that both reader and poet are able to comment upon him. My purpose in this study is really two-fold: first, to trace the development of Auden's new persona that emerged in the fifties; and second, to attempt to explain the effect this new "mask" has had upon the poems.

Contents

I

"A Change of Heart"

W. H. AUDEN'S FATHER was a doctor and his mother a
nurse. Both of his grandfathers and his four uncles
were Anglican clergymen. Auden's earliest interests
were geology, machinery, and mining (Christopher
Isherwood describes Auden's childhood playbox as
being "full of thick scientific books on geology and
metals and machines, borrowed from his father's library"),[1] and his specialty at school was biology. While
at Oxford he developed an interest in psychology, and
Stephen Spender describes Auden by the age of twenty-
one as interested in "poetry, psychoanalysis and medi-
cine," with "an extensive knowledge of the theories of
modern psychology, which he used as a means of
understanding himself and dominating his friends."[2]

[1] Christopher Isherwood, *Lions and Shadows* (Norfolk, Conn.:
New Directions, 1947), p. 181.

[2] Stephen Spender, *World Within World* (London: Hamish Hamil-
ton, 1951), p. 54. In an essay entitled "W. H. Auden and His
Poetry" (*Auden: A Collection of Critical Essays*, ed. Monroe K.
Spears [Englewood Cliffs, N.J.: Prentice-Hall, 1964], p. 28), Spender
says:

> Yet Auden's ideas have changed as strikingly as his way of
> life has remained the same. There is a dualistic idea running
> through all his work which encloses it like the sides of a box.
> The idea is Symptom and Cure. Sometimes Auden's poems are
> more symptomatic than curative; sometimes they concentrate
> with an almost salvationist zeal on the idea of a cure. But from
> the early "look shining at / New styles of architecture, a change
> of heart," to the concluding lines of *The Age of Anxiety*:
>
> > In our anguish we struggle
> > To elude Him, to lie to Him, yet His love observes
> > His appalling promise . . .

Throughout the reminiscences of Spender, Isherwood, and C. Day Lewis, young Auden appears in the various hats of doctor, lay analyst, magician, and, at least to Isherwood, "lunatic clergyman." [3] All of these guises share a common concern for helping others, including a desire to teach or instruct. Auden had studied Sigmund Freud, George Groddeck, Homer Lane, and John Layard (as he was later to study Søren Kierkegaard, Reinhold Niebuhr, Charles Williams, and Charles Cochrane) searching for ways to cure the sickness in man and then to pass the gospel on to his friends.[4]

The particular "cure" which he embraced in the twenties was the concept of being "pure-in-heart." [5] In varying ways, Lane, Layard, Groddeck, and Freud all commanded man to "love thyself" (and subsequently to

the preoccupation is the same. The symptoms have to be diagnosed, named, brought into the open, made to weep and confess, that they may be related to the central need of love, leading them to the discipline which is their cure. The symptoms which prove that man needs to love and that "the grossest of his dreams is / No worse than our worship which for the most part / Is so much galimatias to get out of / Knowing our neighbor" have changed very little. The diagnostician Auden is much the same as he was at Oxford.

It is his conception of the Cure which has changed. At one time Love, in the sense of Freudian release from inhibition; at another time a vaguer and more exalted idea of loving; at still another the Social Revolution; and at a yet later stage, Christianity. Essentially the direction of Auden's poetry has been towards the defining of the concept of love.

[3] C. Day Lewis, *The Buried Day* (New York: Harper & Brothers, 1960); Spender, *World Within World;* Isherwood, *Lions and Shadows,* particular pp. 188–189.

[4] Spender writes of Auden at this time: "Self-knowledge, complete lack of inhibition and sense of guilt, and knowledge of others, were essential to the fulfillment of his aims. Unless one knew oneself, one could not know what one wanted and plan to obtain it; guilt and inhibition stood between oneself and the satisfaction of one's needs; knowledge of others was necessary for the purpose of entering realistically into their lives, and fitting one [sic] pattern of oneself into a larger psychological pattern of surrounding people" (*World Within World,* p. 53).

[5] W. H. Auden and Louis MacNeice, *Letters from Iceland* (New York: Random House, 1937), p. 210.

2

extend this love to others) by purging illness and hatred from within where they were grounded in a sense of guilt that must itself be removed.[6] Borrowing tenets from each man, Auden formulated his own moral system and set about trying to teach it through writing and personal example. As a consequence, poetry (which he was already writing) became a way of teaching. He says in the introduction to *The Poet's Tongue*:

> The psychologist maintains that poetry is a neurotic symptom, an attempt to compensate by phantasy for a failure to meet reality. We must tell him that phantasy is only the beginning of writing; that, on the contrary, like psychology, poetry is a struggle to reconcile the unwilling subject and object; in fact, that since psychological truth depends so largely on context, poetry, the parabolic approach, is the only adequate medium for psychology.[7]

The effect of Auden's beliefs on his poetry becomes quite clear in one poem from the twenties: the prayer which concludes *Poems: 1930*, and which was later ti-

[6] Isherwood, in *Lions and Shadows*, p. 300, paraphrases a letter from Barnard (Layard) to Weston (Auden). It says (in part):
> Every disease, Lane had taught, is in itself a cure—if we know how to take it. There is only one sin; disobedience to the inner law of our own nature. The results of this disobedience show themselves in crime or in disease; but the disobedience is never, in the first place, our own fault—it is the fault of those who teach us, as children, to control God (our desires) instead of giving Him room to grow. The whole problem, when dealing with a patient, is to find out which of all the conflicting things inside him is God, and which is the Devil. And the one sure guide is that God appears always unreasonable, while the Devil appears always to be noble and right. God appears unreasonable because He has been put in prison and driven wild. The Devil is conscious control, and is, therefore, reasonable and sane."

[7] W. H. Auden and John Garrett, eds., *The Poet's Tongue* (London: G. Bell & Sons, 1935), p. ix.

tled "Petition" in *The Collected Poetry of W. H. Auden*:

Sir, no man's enemy, forgiving all
But will its negative inversion, be prodigal:
Send to us power and light, a sovereign touch
Curing the intolerable neural itch,
The exhaustion of weaning, the liar's quinsy,
And the distortions of ingrown virginity.
Prohibit sharply the rehearsed response
And gradually correct the coward's stance;
Cover in time with beams those in retreat
That, spotted, they turn though the reverse were great;
Publish each healer that in city lives
Or country house at the end of drives;
Harrow the house of the dead; look shining at
New styles of architecture, a change of heart.[8]

The first word of the poem, "Sir," by its very indefiniteness introduces the obscurity which so perplexed Cleanth Brooks.[9] Yet this indefiniteness is one of the poem's most effective characteristics. "Sir" may be a form of deity, since the poem is after all a prayer. But it

[8] W. H. Auden, *The Collected Poetry of W. H. Auden* (New York: Random House, 1945), pp. 110–111.

[9] Cleanth Brooks, in *Modern Poetry and the Tradition* (Chapel Hill: University of North Carolina Press, 1939), pp. 1–3, caused a minor controversy by using "Petition" as an example of difficult poetry. In the magazine *Explicator*, III, 5 (March 1945), 38, Wallace Cable Brown attempted to explain the poem by treating "Sir" as God the Father being cavalierly addressed. Then two months later *Explicator*, III, 7 (May 1945), 51, carried the replies of D. A. Robertson, Jr., Hallett Smith, and W. K. Wimsatt, Jr., to the comments of Brooks and Brown. Robertson mentioned the importance of the influence of Lane and Hopkins ("I that spend, / Sir, life upon thy cause"); Smith stated a belief that "Sir" was God the Uncle rather than God the Father; and Wimsatt, in a genuine attempt to explicate the poem, tried to deal with its underlying ideas. He said in part: "The evils of human life are thought of less as culpable sins than as diseases or mistakes, the cure for which is the kind of knowledge of soul afforded by the new sciences of psychology and psychiatry."

4

would seem to be a lay prayer, directed not so much outwardly as inwardly. "Sir" may be a god or a school-master, a father or a ruler ("a sovereign touch"), or simply anyone with power and authority. What *is* significant about this "Sir" is that he is "no man's enemy." Auden, like the others of his generation, was caught up in the chaos between the wars. As children during the First World War, he and his friends took many of the ideas for their childhood games from the alignment and opposition of forces in wartime. As Auden matured, he began to notice the same oppositions in society: rich against poor for instance, with his own class—the bourgeoisie—trapped stupidly in the middle. His early poetry is filled with frontiers or borders between enemies; there is a constant we-they opposition. If one is not a friend, he must be a foe.[10] But not "Sir." He does not take sides and is capable of "forgiving all." All, that is, save one thing: "will its negative inversion." The self-destructive impulse, the death wish, is the only unforgivable sin because it is a symptom of the total misuse of the power of mind over body.[11] The other psychological ills of man ("the intolerable neural itch, / The exhaustion of weaning, the liar's quinsy, / . . . ingrown virginity") can be forgiven and cured if man will only recognize their existence.[12] For "Sir" can send "power and light," and even "Cover in time with beams those in retreat / That, spotted, they turn though the reverse were great." The idea of "power and light" here is a complex one. It contains both the implication of man-kind's material advance as shown in the example of the

---

[10] See Isherwood, *Lions and Shadows,* chapters II and III.

[11] Spender says of Auden, in *World Within World,* p. 62: "He walked very fast on flat feet, with striding angular movements of his arms and legs and jerkings up of his head. Once he had been told by a doctor that he must walk as little as possible, so he immediately began going for thirty-mile walks. He had a theory that the body is controlled by the mind. He would explain a headache, a cold, or sore throat in what are now called 'psychosomatic' terms."

[12] See Isherwood, *Lions and Shadows,* pp. 213–217, 301–304, with regard to Auden on psychological diseases.

modern power company, and the implication of an advance in mental well-being made possible through the development of modern psychology. The image of "those in retreat" (those who refuse to face themselves or their world in this new "light") being "spotted" brings these ideas together. If these frightened creatures are stopped in time they can be turned in the right direction, to the healers' doors, whether in city or in country. These healers, of whom Homer Lane would seem to be a good prototype, are teachers, capable of showing through example that a "change of heart" (gaining the ability to love both oneself and others) can effect "New styles of architecture."

"Petition" is a poem filled with possibility. At its center is the belief that man *is* capable of building a New Jerusalem,[13] using the "power and light" of progress and insight. The nature of "Sir," then, becomes quite clear by the end of the poem. "No man's enemy," he stands for all that is positive and possible; he is the manifestation of the existence of a cure, not the cure itself but a guiding spirit for reaching it.

The ideas and images of "Petition" give a good picture of Auden as he entered the 1930s. He believed in the possibility of reform in both the individual and society. He believed that man could be good if purged of his self-induced ills, and that society could be healed and a New Jerusalem brought about. He believed in the healing powers of psychology and in material advancement, and he used images from both to construct his poems. Finally, he viewed himself and his friends as teachers, his poems as vehicles for teaching, and mankind as capable of being taught.

[13] Spender, in "W. H. Auden and His Poetry," p. 29, says: "Auden . . . puts himself on the side of Blake, D. H. Lawrence, and other English mystics, with their highly individualistic philosophies, who spent their creative energy in protesting against the smugness of England. Their protest comes from a bitter love of their country and a deep faith that a New Jerusalem could be built on this island if only the English would stop being so English."

6

In *World Within World* (p. 202), Spender writes about the thirties:

> In the 1920's there had been a generation of American writers—Scott Fitzgerald, Ernest Hemingway, Malcolm Cowley, and some others— whom Gertrude Stein had called the Lost Generation. We anti-Fascist writers of what has been called the Pink Decade were not, in any obvious sense, a lost generation. But we were divided between our literary vocation and an urge to save the world from Fascism. We were the Divided Generation of Hamlets who found the world out of joint and failed to set it right.
>
> The call we heard was by no means so absurd as it may sound to a later generation. For in those days Japan still could have been prevented from invading Manchuria, Hitler could have been thrown out of power at the time of the Anschluss or the invasion of the Rhineland, the Spanish Republic could have been saved. If any of these opportunities had been seized, there would have been no terrible totalitarian war followed by a totalitarian peace: the one thing required then was a conscience extending far beyond the existing circles of professional politicians in the democracies, to the people. This deeply awakened public conscience could have forced Britain, France, and perhaps even the United States, to take the stand necessary to prevent war.

The "if" of Spender's recollection was what Auden believed to be possible during the 1920s and the early 1930s, but quite a bit happened or did not happen during the 1930s to Auden and to the world. Some indication of the way in which the decade's events affected the man may be gained from an examination of a poem written roughly ten years after "Petition": "September 1, 1939."

I sit in one of the dives
On Fifty-second Street
Uncertain and afraid
As the clever hopes expire
Of a low dishonest decade:
Waves of anger and fear
Circulate over the bright
And darkened lands of the earth,
Obsessing our private lives;
The unmentionable odour of death
Offends the September night.

Accurate scholarship can
Unearth the whole offense
From Luther until now
That has driven a culture mad,
Find what occurred at Linz,
What huge imago made
A psychopathic god:
I and the public know
What all schoolchildren learn,
Those to whom evil is done
Do evil in return.

Exiled Thucydides knew
All that a speech can say
About democracy,
And what dictators do,
The elderly rubbish they talk
To an apathetic grave;
Analyzed all in his book,
The enlightenment driven away,
The habit-forming pain,
Mismanagement and grief:
We must suffer them all again.

Into this neutral air
Where blind skyscrapers use

Their full height to proclaim
The strength of Collective Man,
Each language pours its vain
Competitive excuse:
But who can live for long
In an euphoric dream;
Out of the mirror they stare,
Imperialism's face
And the international wrong.

Faces along the bar
Cling to their average day:
The lights must never go out,
The music must always play,
All the conventions conspire
To make this fort assume
The furniture of home;
Lest we should see where we are,
Lost in a haunted wood,
Children afraid of the night
Who have never been happy or good.

The windiest militant trash
Important Persons shout
Is not so crude as our wish:
What mad Nijinsky wrote
About Diaghilev
Is true of the normal heart;
For the error bred in the bone
Of each woman and each man
Craves what it cannot have,
Not universal love
But to be loved alone.

From the conservative dark
Into the ethical life
The dense commuters come,

Repeating their morning vow;
"I *will* be true to the wife,
I'll concentrate more on my work,"
And helpless governors wake
To resume their compulsory game:
Who can release them now,
Who can reach the deaf,
Who can speak for the dumb?

Defenceless under the night
Our world in stupor lies;
Yet, dotted everywhere,
Ironic points of light
Flash out wherever the Just
Exchange their messages:
May I, composed like them
Of Eros and of dust,
Beleaguered by the same
Negation and despair,
Show an affirming flame.[14]

"September 1, 1939" is, like "Petition," a type of
prayer, but similarities between the two poems cease
there, where they begin. If the tone of "Petition" is one
of pride in possibility, the tone of "September 1, 1939"
is one of humility in failure. Whereas in "Petition" the
emphasis is on hope for a future of "cured" men in a
"cured" society, here it is clearly on the progression of
human sin and weakness from the past to the present,
culminating now when "The unmentionable odour of
death / Offends the September night." In Auden's early
poems the purity of the distant, often Nordic, past is
contrasted with the confusion of the present and the
possibilities of the future. But in "September 1, 1939"
the past offers no contrasts; history provides no lessons,
no errors future generations can correct, for

[14] Auden, *Collected Poetry*, pp. 57–59.

> Exiled Thucydides knew
> All that a speech can say
> About Democracy.

The idea of a New Jerusalem is foolish, no more than "an euphoric dream," for each time we attempt to offer excuses for the past or promises for the future we are forced to examine ourselves and then:

> Out of the mirror they stare,
> Imperialism's face
> And the international wrong.

Mankind has made a mess of things, yet to Auden, at this time, recognition of that fact is really meaningless since there is nothing man can do to cure his ills. The sickness is nothing so simple as "liar's quinsy" or the "coward's stance"; it is "the error bred in the bone" which leads mankind to crave

> . . . what it cannot have,
> Not universal love
> But to be loved alone.

The "error" is selfishness, selfishness of a grotesque and self-consuming nature, and it is incurable. So long as man is flesh, composed "Of Eros and of dust," the "error bred in the bone" will be an essential characteristic of his nature, part of the legacy to which he is heir. Because of this, history merely repeats itself; the "New styles of architecture" are only "blind skyscrapers," and "a change of heart" in mankind proves to be an illusion: we are but "Children afraid of the night / Who have never been happy or good." [15]
Yet in spite of the destruction of the dream envi-

[15] Auden says elsewhere, in "Nature, History and Poetry," *Thought*, XXV, 98 (September 1950), that "The historical world is a fallen world, i.e., though it is good that it exists, the way in which it exists is evil, being full of unfreedom and disorder."

sioned in "Petition," all is not lost. "Uncertain and afraid" though he is, man still possesses the power to choose.[16] To illustrate this, Auden sets the poem in a bar (a setting he later uses more elaborately in *The Age of Anxiety*). A bar offers, at least, the illusion of possibility or, more correctly, the illusion of the possibility of escape. There men may "Cling to their average day," demanding that "The lights must never go out, / The music must always play." The way of the bar is one choice—man tries to avoid facing the surrounding darkness by hiding himself in an artificial light.

The other choice is not so easy to make. It involves seeing oneself and one's world as they really are, looking into the night and the "haunted wood" and, instead of turning away in fear, offering an "affirming flame." This flame is far different from the "power and light" or the "beams" of "Petition." It is not curative. It is not universal. Yet these small flames are "dotted everywhere, / Ironic points of light." They are the signals of those whom Auden terms "the Just." These "Just," it would seem, are the men who are able to acknowledge their "errors," recognize the "Negation and despair," and still strive towards an affirmation of life. They

---

[16] When "September 1, 1939" first appeared (both in *The New Republic*, October 18, 1939, and in *Another Time* [New York: Random House, 1940]), it contained a stanza which Auden chose to eliminate when the poem was reprinted in *Collected Poetry*. The stanza was the eighth (penultimate) and went:

All I have is a voice	There is no such thing as the State
To undo the folded lie,	And no one exists alone;
The romantic lie in the brain	Hunger allows no choice
Of the sensual man-in-the-street	To the citizens or the police;
And the lie of Authority	We must love one another or die.
Whose buildings grope the sky:	

The omission both puzzled and angered Beach, who said: "This eighth stanza marks the crux of the whole matter" (*The Making of Auden Canon* [Minneapolis: University of Minnesota Press, 1957], p. 51). He felt that Auden left it out because it was not religious enough. This may be so, but it seems more likely that Auden eliminated it because it was too explicit ("We must love one another or die"), reducing the choice at the heart of the poem to no choice at all.

know that mankind is unredeemable as "Defenceless under the night / Our world in stupor lies," and yet, ironically, they must affirm.

By placing "Petition" and "September 1, 1939" side by side, we get a very clear idea of the change Auden experienced in the decade separating their composition. "Petition" shows us a world to come, a world of light, of good people in a bright, shining city. "September 1, 1939" shows us the world of then, now, and to come, a world blanketed by eternal darkness, with tiny dots of light, like stars, punctuating the night.

Whether or not Auden had returned to Christianity at the time of the composition of "September 1, 1939" is a matter of some debate. It would appear, particularly from evidence in the original penultimate stanza which was deleted from the version reprinted in *The Collected Poetry*, that he had not. Rather, he was caught between his old humanistic beliefs and his new feeling that these were false; and he had not as yet found a complete, new system to replace the old.

In an untitled essay in a collection edited by James A. Pike, *Modern Canterbury Pilgrims*, Auden gives a detailed account of precisely what happened to him during the thirties. He says, in part:

> The various "kerygmas," of Blake, of Lawrence, of Freud, of Marx, to which, along with most middle-class intellectuals of my generation, I paid attention between twenty and thirty, had one thing in common. They were all Christian heresies; that is to say, one cannot imagine their coming into existence except in a civilization which claimed to be based, religiously, on belief that the Word was made flesh and dwelt among us, and that, in consequence, matter, the natural order, is real and redeemable, not a shadowy appearance or the cause of evil, and historical time is real and significant, not meaningless or an endless series of cycles. . . .

What was one looking for at the time? Nothing is more difficult to recall than past assumptions, but I think the state of mind among most of my contemporaries was somewhat as follows. We assumed that there was only one outlook on life conceivable among civilized people, the liberal humanism in which all of us had been brought up, whether we came from Christian or agnostic homes (English liberalism had never been anti-clerical like its Continental brother).

To this the theological question seemed irrelevant since such values as freedom of person, equal justice for all, respect for the rights of others, etc., were self-evident truths. However, the liberal humanism of the past had failed to produce the universal peace and prosperity it promised, failed even to prevent a World War. What had it overlooked? The subconscious, said Freud; the means of production, said Marx. Liberalism was not to be superseded; it was to be made effective instead of self-defeating.

Then the Nazis came to power in Germany. The Communists had said that one must hate and destroy some of one's neighbors now in order to create a world in which nobody would be able to help loving his neighbors tomorrow. They had attacked Christianity and all religions on the ground that, so long as people are taught to love a non-existent God, they will ignore the material obstacles to human brotherhood. The novelty and shock of the Nazis was that they made no pretense of believing in justice and liberty for all, and attacked Christianity on the grounds that to love one's neighbor as oneself was a command fit only for effeminate weaklings, not for the "healthy blood of the master race." Moreover, this utter denial of everything liberalism had ever stood for was arousing wild enthusiasm, not in some remote barbaric land outside the pale, but in one of the most highly educated countries in Europe, a country one knew well and where one had many friends. Confronted by such a phenomenon, it was impossible any longer to believe that the values of liberal humanism were self-evident. Unless one was prepared to take a relativistic view that all values are a matter of personal taste, one could hardly avoid asking the question: "If, as I am convinced, the Nazis are wrong and we are right, what is it that validates our values and invalidates theirs? . . ."

Shortly afterwards, in a publisher's office, I met an Anglican layman, and for the first time in my life felt myself in the presence of personal sanctity. I had met many good people before who made me feel ashamed of my own shortcomings, but in the presence of this man—we never discussed anything but literary business—I did not feel ashamed. I felt transformed into a person who was incapable of doing or thinking anything base or unloving. (I later discovered that he had had a similar effect on many other people.)

So, presently, I started to read some theological works, Kierkegaard in particular, and began going, in a tentative and experimental sort of way, to church. And then, providentially—for the occupational disease of poets is frivolity—I was forced to know in person what it is like to feel oneself the prey of demonic powers, in both the Greek and the Christian sense, stripped of self-control and self-respect, behaving like a ham actor in a Strindberg play.

Much as I owe to Kierkegaard—among many other virtues, he has the talent, invaluable in a preacher to the Greeks, of making Christianity sound bohemian—I cannot let this occasion pass without commenting upon what seems to be his great limitation, a limitation which characterizes

Protestantism generally. A planetary visitor might read through the whole of his voluminous works without discovering that human beings are not ghosts but have bodies of flesh and blood . . . and it is with this body, with faith or without it, that all good works are done.

As a spirit, a conscious person endowed with free will, every man has, through faith and grace, a unique "existential" relation to God, and few since St. Augustine have described this relation more profoundly than Kierkegaard. But every man has a second relation to God which is neither unique nor existential: as a creature composed of matter, as a biological organism, every man, in common with everything else in the universe, is related by necessity to the God who created that universe and saw that it was good, for the laws of nature to which, whether he likes it or not, he must conform are of divine origin.[17]

There are many interesting revelations in this short essay. First there is the recognition and acceptance of the idea that Marx, Freud, Lawrence, and Blake, who had greatly influenced Auden's early thought and work, were really Christian heretics—that is, their protests formed a dialectic within the Christian context. Then Kierkegaard, whose ideas seem to dominate Auden's work of the forties, is placed in proper perspective in terms of influence. Much has been written about Kierkegaard's influence on Auden, and it is not the purpose of this study to belabor the subject further, but it is interesting to note that although Auden recognizes the profundity of Kierkegaard's conception of the spiritual relationship between man and God, he is more than a little disturbed that Kierkegaard seems to dismiss a second and, to Auden, equally significant relation—that of

[17] James A. Pike, ed., *Modern Canterbury Pilgrims* (New York: Morehouse–Graham, 1956), pp. 32–43.

16

man as matter to God as Maker. Auden claims that this is Kierkegaard's "great limitation," for "it is with this body, with faith or without it, that all good works are done."

This concern with man as body as well as spirit leads directly to the man who, I feel, has had the greatest influence on Auden's development from the time he met him to the present day: the unidentified "Anglican layman." This was Charles Williams, and Auden says a great deal about both the man and his work in an introduction which he wrote to a reprint, in 1956, of Williams' *The Descent of the Dove*:

> I have met great and good men in whose presence one was conscious of one's own littleness; Charles Williams' effect on me and on others with whom I have spoken was quite different: in his company one felt twice as intelligent and infinitely nicer than, out of it, one knew oneself to be. It wasn't simply that he was a sympathetic listener— he talked a lot and he talked well—but, more than anyone else I have ever known, he gave himself completely to the company that he was in . . . any conversation with Charles Williams, no matter how trivial and impersonal the topic was, was a genuine dialogue.
>
> When, later, I began to read his books, I realized why this was so; the basic theme which runs through all of them is a doctrine of exchange and substitution, a way of life by which, it was clear, he himself lived.
>
> The doctrine might be briefly summarized as follows: the first law of the spiritual universe, the Real City, is that nobody can carry his own burden; he only can, and therefore he must, carry someone else's. Whose burden in particular he should carry is up to him to decide.
>
> This has nothing to do with the self-righteous at-

titude I once heard expressed in a parody of a sermon: "We are all here on earth to help others; what on earth the others are here for I don't know." One-sided exchange is a contradiction. Choosing to bear another's burden involves at the same time permitting another to carry one's own, and this may well be the harder choice, just as it is usually easier to forgive than be forgiven. The motto of the City is: "your life and death are with your neighbour" and this co-inherence is not limited to contemporaries, for it includes the already dead and the as yet unborn. . . .

I believe that Charles Williams would have gone even further and said that, in fact, there is no such thing as one's own cross; the troubles that one thinks of, and too often resents as one's own, may well be another's, and, once this is realized, they become tolerable.[18]

In the late 1920s, personal contact with John Layard had brought Auden an awareness of the ideas of Homer Lane and had given him a living example of their virtues; this helped to coalesce certain ideas that Auden already held into a broader, more meaningful pattern— a "life style." [19] But by the time Auden met Williams, the notion of healing oneself and then one's society had ceased being credible to him. He was in a state of confusion; he was without a world view. Meeting Williams

[18] Charles Williams, *The Descent of the Dove* (New York: Meridian Books, 1956), pp. v–vii.

[19] Isherwood (*Lions and Shadows*, p. 299) recalls: "But the most important experience of Weston's Berlin visit had had nothing to do with Germany or the Germans at all. One evening, in a cafe, he had got into conversation with a stranger, an Englishman named Barnard. This Mr. Barnard—himself an anthropologist and a most remarkable man from all accounts—had first told Weston about the great psychologist, Homer Lane. Barnard had been a patient and pupil of Lane's, and now, since the master's death, he was one of the very few people really qualified to spread Lane's teachings and carry on his work. In Weston, he had found an intelligent listener who became, overnight, an enthusiastic disciple."

changed all that and started Auden on the way to reconversion. The compelling trait that Williams possessed—and it was an extremely important one in a climate of what seemed to Auden to be universal moral anarchy—was that of being a truly good man. Williams actually lived what he taught, and, to Auden, this was nothing short of miraculous. When Auden went from the man to his writings, he discovered, as did T. S. Eliot, that Williams was "wholly the same man in his life and in his writings." The goodness in Williams was the doctrine of substitution realized; the feeling Auden had in his presence was that of a companion in the coinherence.

Auden then began reading Kierkegaard, Neibuhr, Paul Tillich, and Cochrane, and his writing began to show new influences. (The hesitant "New Year Letter," for instance, appears almost a pastiche of Williams and Kierkegaard, and the character of Prospero in *The Sea and the Mirror* speaks in what is almost a Kierkegaardian paraphrase.) It is his writing, in fact, that gives evidence of the battle Auden was waging with himself throughout the forties not only to believe in Williams' idea of substitution but to live it as well. The long poems of this decade are filled with the loneliness of this struggle. The old liberal "voice" of the thirties had vanished, and in the search for a new one Auden experimented. He employed new stylistic devices (as in *The Sea and the Mirror*); contrasted old voices with new (as in the characters Simeon and Herod in *For the Time Being*); and worked on the development of a new persona, which ranged from the unsure but penitent intellectual we see in Caliban to the Narrator of *For the Time Being*, and, finally, to the Kierkegaardian failure, Malin, of *The Age of Anxiety*. Auden was really searching for a voice quite different from that of either Caliban or Malin. As a consequence, the long poems of this period seem to be poems Auden *had* to write rather than poems he *wanted* to write. They are works of tran-

19

sition, attempts to understand the incredible gap between a Hitler and a Williams. We do not know when Auden the man began to understand how to bridge this chasm, but we do know when Auden the poet found the artistic means to give form to his new beliefs. It occurs in Auden's major work of the fifties, "Horae Canonicae," his artistic testimony not only to his acceptance and understanding of Williams' ideas, but also to his own joining of the "companions of the co-inherence." It deals with the first and greatest of all the substitutions, Christ's sacrifice on the Cross, which is seen through the eyes of a gentle, humble, ordinary man: Auden's new persona.

The journey from "September 1, 1939" to "Horae Canonicae" and beyond to the light, personal poems of *About the House* is an interesting one because the poems written along the way give a very clear picture of man-as-poet struggling to create with honesty, objectivity, and clarity of voice.

II

The Sea and the Mirror

The Sea and the Mirror (1944) is based upon Shakespeare's *The Tempest;* in fact, its subtitle is "A Commentary on Shakespeare's *The Tempest.*" However, the work is not an attempt at explication, or a tribute, but stems instead from Auden's critical interpretation of the position Shakespeare had taken regarding the central philosophical issue of that play.[1] As Auden himself says: "The Tempest seems to me a manichean work, not because it shows the relation of Nature to Spirit as one of conflict and hostility, which in fallen man it is, but because it puts the blame for this upon Nature and makes the Spirit innocent."[2] Viewed in this light, *The Sea and the Mirror* is an attempt on Auden's part to correct the heresy and make *The Tempest* orthodox.

It is, of course, much more. Many critics maintain that it is Auden's masterpiece, while others find it even more irritating than Auden found *The Tempest.*[3] It is a puzzling work. By far the most technically complicated

[1] W. H. Auden, *The Dyer's Hand* (New York: Random House, 1962), pp. 128–134. See also Stephen Spender, *Poetry Since 1939*, British Council Pamphlet (London: Longmans, Green, 1946), p. 30: "To Auden, *The Tempest* has always appeared to be the mystery play in which Shakespeare came nearest to expressing his philosophy in characters who have a symbolic significance."

[2] *The Dyer's Hand*, p. 130.

[3] Joseph Beach says that "More than half of 'The Sea and the Mirror' (Caliban to the Audience) is a long-winded disquisition in prose on (as I understand it) literary-art-in-an-age-of-naturalistic-unbelief" (*The Making of the Auden Canon*, p. 207). See also Randall Jarrell, "Freud to Paul: The Stages of Auden's Ideology," *The Partisan Review*, XII (Fall, 1945), 437–457.

of all of Auden's poetry, it is also, perhaps because of its complexity, one of his most difficult works ideationally.

One approach towards understanding *The Sea and the Mirror* is to consider it as drama. *The Sea and the Mirror* is a modern sequel to *The Tempest*. It is, as a play, perhaps closer to Brecht than to Shakespeare, for its dramatic effect depends to a great extent upon the relationship of the audience to the drama. The audience must participate in *The Sea and the Mirror,* and the movement of the poem from section to section is dependent upon this participation.

When I say that *The Sea and the Mirror* is drama, I do not mean that it need actually be staged. But I do mean that the reader must consider himself as part of an audience and imaginatively "stage" the work; that is, allow himself to *see* the situation as well as follow the movement of the ideas.

What Auden has tried to do in *The Sea and the Mirror* is to give life to an extremely complex system of metaphors. Instead of merely saying, as one would in an essay, that our life is to God as a stage production is to our life, he has tried to show this in the dramatic relationship of the elements of theater: actor, character, Author, Stage Manager, Critic, audience.

It would seem that Auden chose *The Tempest* because it is an "open-ended" play. Even though it is set in an almost ideal metaphoric setting, the isolation of an island, it is not perfectly resolved. Caliban and Ariel are left free, but their lives are directionless. And Prospero himself, having abandoned his magic, turns to the audience for assistance. Shakespeare begins with Prospero as artist/god, but then Prospero quits. It is at this point that Auden begins his drama, showing Shakespeare's characters with the island and its god no more, caught up (as we all are) in the sea of life once again. We know the past of each character; we know the present; Auden gives us their plans for the future.

Auden opens *The Sea and the Mirror* with a prefatory speech delivered by the Stage Manager of a company that has just performed *The Tempest* to a group of Critics seated in the audience. The purpose of this speech is to set the scene for what is to follow, to give the reader an imaginative point from which to see the situation that Auden wishes to create. If we begin an examination of *The Sea and the Mirror* with an attempt to discover the nature of this scene and the characters populating it, we shall eliminate many of the problems which arise from the complex structure of the work.

It is important, first of all, that Auden chooses to begin with the Stage Manager, rather than the Producer, Author, or Director. Once the performance of a play has begun, the jobs of the Producer, Author, and Director are completed. If it is an opening night (and since the Critics are present it would appear that it is), the three of them would be "out front" evaluating audience reaction and possible weaknesses in the production. It is the Stage Manager who *runs* the performance once it has begun. He need not be a philosopher, nor a creative man, but he must be an organizer. It is his job to see that everyone and everything are in the right places at the right times as previously established by the Author or Director. He has the authority and the responsibility for the elimination of mechanical error in the performance, and it is his job to make sure that there are no surprises, to make sure that the art is not life. So, when the Stage Manager parts the curtains after the performance to address the Critics, he cannot be blamed for any lack of imagination from which the performance may have suffered, but only for mechanical errors. These he may apologize for with a simple "I'm sorry, it won't happen next time," something no author or director could say with clear conscience.

The Stage Manager is, then, if the performance is free from chance error, the least open to serious criticism of all those associated with the production. He may step out, comment on the execution of the production, and move on to other things—which is what Auden has him do.

When he appears before the curtain, his job is done, the performance completed. The job of the Critics is really just beginning. They have seen the show, received and reacted to impressions. Now they must give form to these reactions, communicable form that may serve as a guide to others. This guide should be more than just value judgment; it should be an explanation of the work, an attempt to relate the performance to life, to give answers to the problems posed by the work. The critic, when he leaves the theater, goes home to *think* about what he has seen. During a performance he may respond emotionally with the rest of the audience, but after the show he must make sense out of it.

In the first stanza, the Stage Manager recapitulates the action of a show and the audience reaction to it.

> The aged catch their breath,
> For the nonchalant couple go
> Waltzing across the tightrope
> As if there were no death
> Or hope of falling down;
> The wounded cry as the clown
> Doubles his meaning, and O
> How the dear little children laugh
> When the drums roll and the lovely
> Lady is sawn in half.[4]

It would seem that he is describing not *The Tempest*, but rather a circus, the least coherently formed and least intellectual of all entertainments and, at the same time, the least illusory and the closest to life. "The aged catch their breath" because there is danger in the high-wire act, the performers act as themselves, not as characters in a play. The excitement is there because of "the

[4] Auden, *Collected Poetry*, p. 351.

nonchalant couple . . . / Waltzing" in spite of the danger.

Aside from the visual effect of this first, circus image, there is a further symbolic effect. The tightrope has been used often by Auden (as it is used later in *The Sea and the Mirror* in Alonzo's speech) as a symbol for man's passage through life; [5] thus the aged, who have almost completed their journey, "catch their breath" at the carefree attitude of the couple acting "As if there were no death."

Death is frightening, particularly to the aged, because man does not know what comes next. Yet, in the next line, Auden uses the word "hope" instead of "fear." It would appear that to the aged, looking back along their own tightrope journeys, the fear of death is coupled with the wish for death, an end to the anxiety of the journey, a "hope of falling down."

"The aged catch their breath" because they contrast the waltzing couple's nonchalance with their own knowledge of the realities of "this world of fact." They bring the worlds of art and life together, expecting from art the same high seriousness that life—at least from their point of view—possesses. There is no purgation, for they expect the actors to receive what they, the audience, would receive.

The same attitude toward the relationship between life and art is shown in the Stage Manager's second example, "The wounded" crying "as the clown / Doubles his meaning." Here "The wounded," perhaps the middle-aged who are acutely aware that there is no return in time, expect escape but find in the double entendre an example or situation too close to their own lives, a poking fun at what is painful in life. Only in the inno-

[5] For an example of this, see "Many Happy Returns" (*Collected Poetry*, p. 71), the last stanza of which reads:

Tao is a tightrope,   Intellectual talents
So to keep your balance,   With a sensual gusto,
May you always, Johnny,   The Socratic Doubt with
    Manage to combine   The Socratic Sign.

cence of the children is escape to be found. They laugh when "the lovely / Lady is sawn in half" because they have not been in the situation themselves before, are not in it now, and cannot conceive of the possibility of its occurrence.

This is the scene presented to the Critics by the Stage Manager; he is asking them to be aware of the audience as well as the show. What Auden is asking us to do is to be aware from the very beginning of *The Sea and the Mirror* of the possibilities inherent in the relationship between life and art, to be aware of the narrow boundary between illusion and reality. He asks us, in short, to try to place ourselves in the position of the Critics and to think about what we see.

Once the Stage Manager has set the scene, he moves directly to the problem of man's existence. Since it is his job to eliminate real surprise while maintaining the illusion of surprise, it is only natural that he should begin his discussion of existence in theatrical terms. As a result, the scientist's nonaccidental, mechanical universe becomes one in which

> . . . the ghosts who haunt our lives
> Are handy with mirrors and wire.

This is a purely theatrical image of the universe and is applicable to what occurs backstage; in the theater the Stage Manager controls the "ghosts" who are never seen by the audience but whose handiness with mirrors and wire is essential to the completeness of the illusion. There is a solid natural order behind all things.

"But," inquires the Stage Manager, "how does one think up a habit?" How does rational order explain the completely irrational? The Stage Manager's notion of existence would seem to be this: the irrational, unconscious fears and needs of human beings, before which reason pales, permit only "our wonder, our terror" to remain.

26

So much for one answer to the problem of existence. No matter how perfectly executed we believe the backstage operations of our lives to be, the fact of living still fills us with anxiety. The Stage Manager then presents us with a different view; no longer backstage, we are asked to look at the work of art itself. We receive a purgative benefit from watching and are left "wet with sympathy." We feel better, say "Thanks for the evening." But the "thanks" are only for one evening; the purgation is illusory; we are still powerless to fill

> The lion's mouth whose hunger
> No metaphors can fill.

The "lion's mouth" is the anxiety of existence ("the Shadow" as Eliot termed it in "The Hollow Men"). It is the inability of man to make the move from the unconfident "Shall I?" to the self-confident "I Will." The heroes of literature, with all their roaring and dying, are of no use to us here. For the hero has no problem, he is already firmly in the camp of the "I Will"; for him there never was the psychological problem of the lion's mouth. For us there is.

The Stage Manager dismisses the solutions offered by both science and art with unanswerable, almost rhetorical, questions. He says, in effect, "What you say is all very well and good," and then adds, "but what does it have to do with life?"

The Stage Manager concludes his prefatory remarks with a stanza beginning,

> Well, who in his own backyard
> Has not opened his heart to the smiling
> Secret he cannot quote?

The "Well" sets the tone of the Stage Manager's conclusion. After posing questions dealing with the problem at the very core of existence, he verbally shrugs his shoulders and flatly asserts that we have all been through it, even though we cannot talk about it. The use of "Well" closely followed by "Which goes to show that the Bard / Was sober . . ." is a device on the Stage Manager's part to get out of a situation which is too serious to put into words, even if he could find them. As an escape device it works, rendering into platitude the Shakespearean paraphrase which follows [6] and ending the Stage Manager's speech on an ironic note. But this ironic note does not destroy the serious import of what has gone before; on the contrary, it heightens the problem through relief. For what Auden is concerned with in *The Sea and the Mirror*, beyond the discussion of art versus life, is what we do when we discover "That this world of fact we love / Is unsubstantial stuff."

The Stage Manager in his prefatory speech poses the problem of existence as he sees it to the Critics (or the readers). He sets the stage for the action to follow, not only by what he says but by the way in which he says it. He is able to tell us what is wrong with the answers of others, but when it comes to offering a solution himself, he must fall back on saying:

> All the rest is silence
> On the other side of the wall. . . .

In saying it, he clichés it, leaving the Critics dissatisfied but thinking. It is Auden's purpose in the rest of *The Sea and the Mirror* to show other characters, in this case the familiar characters of *The Tempest*, trying to penetrate this silence or offering individual consolations for their inabilities to do so. The Stage Manager, by telling us that the play is over, makes it possible for

[6] The paraphrase is a mixture of Hamlet ("The readiness is all" [V, ii, 210] and "The rest is silence" [V, ii, 345]) and Edgar ("Ripeness is all" [*King Lear*, V, ii, 11]). It would seem that Auden intended to imply a contrast between the attitudes of the two characters, making both attitudes appear inadequate.

the characters to free themselves from the confines of a script which must, since it is art, be complete—begin and end. Once free, the characters are able to move between art and life, to be both characters and actors. By setting the scene, posing the problem, and offering his own way out, the Stage Manager also frees the audience from the expectation of a solution, making the audience (in the role of Critic) an active participant in what is to come.

In the first speech of the characters, Prospero addresses Ariel, explaining what he plans to do and why he wants to do it. It is in Prospero's speech that the meaning of the Stage Manager's solution begins to become clear. "The smiling / Secret" revealed to man in the privacy of "his own backyard" is that he is going to die. Prospero, having known immortality, or the illusion of it, under Ariel's influence, is deliberately setting out on a voyage towards death. By giving up his art "To the silent dissolution of the sea," he is admitting that, for man, art or magic or any illusion is but delusion and represents an attempt to escape from real life, from "The gross insult of being a mere one among many." [7] What Prospero has come to realize is best summed up by his own seemingly simple statement to Ariel: "I am that I am." Not *what* but *that*. Prospero is no longer concerned with position or title, but with the fact of existence. The words of God to Moses which Prospero speaks can have two meanings for him: "I am that (which) I am," that object which you perceive, nothing more or less; and "I am that (because) I am," I exist because I exist. Both meanings direct one's attention to a particular object at a particular place in a par-

[7] Prospero has felt, as Auden says elsewhere (*The Dyer's Hand*, p. 104), that "When I consider others I can easily believe that their bodies express their personalities and that the two are inseparable. But it is impossible for me not to feel that my body is other than I, that I inhabit it like a house, and that my face is a mask which, with or without my consent, conceals my real nature from others."

ticular moment of time. Prospero has, by making this simple statement, locked himself firmly into historical time, into

. . . a universe where time is not foreshortened,
No animals talk, and there is neither floating nor flying.

In short, Prospero has decided to become a man.

Prospero, as we see him here, is, perhaps, Auden's ideal questor. Like Eliot's Tiresias, Prospero has knowledge; he has—through the power of illusion—seen the Land of Oz, has, in fact, like Dorothy, been there. But Prospero is "glad that I did not recover my dukedom till / I do not want it." His desire is not to recapture the past, but to find a place from which he can begin his quest, "Sailing alone, out over seventy thousand fathoms."

The Stage Manager was unable to talk about the "smiling / Secret" directly and so avoided it by saying that "the rest is silence." It is this silence that the Stage Manager is not prepared to face, and the way in which he talks about it is an attempt to be ironic. Prospero, on the other hand, is earnestly ready to begin.

The knowledge which Prospero possessed and upon which he had based his life was a knowledge of the methods of escape from life, a way in which to show, as he puts it, that "I was not what I seemed." He used his art to get away from his own mortality, feeling secure in his belief in himself as ultimately moral and as ultimately alone. His dicti were those of a god: "To hate nothing and ask nothing for its love." Both of these he broke, because, as he discovered, he placed himself not as an isolated man among men, but as an isolated man *above* men. Prospero exchanged life for the "mirror of art," believing that in this mirror he would see things idealized, see himself as he wished to be; but, when he looked into the mirror of Ariel's "calm eyes," he saw Caliban and realized that, far from getting an idealized picture from the mirror, "all we are not stares back at what we are." [8]

Prospero realized that the real journey of life begins not with the wish or the mirror, but with the silence of the self. One's "own backyard" is oneself alone, facing existence without illusion. When Prospero asks Ariel:

> *O brilliantly, lightly,*
> *Of separation,*
> *Of bodies and death,*
> *Unanxious one, sing*
> *To man, meaning me,*
> *As now, meaning always,*
> *In love or out,*
> *Whatever that mean,*
> *Trembling he takes*
> *The silent passage*
> *Into discomfort,*

the song he wants is not illusory but real, "Of separation, / Of bodies and death." Regardless of the consequences, Prospero feels he can stand no more illusion.

Prospero's soliloquy is followed by part two of the main body of *The Sea and the Mirror* entitled "The Supporting Cast, Sotto Voce." This section consists of speeches by the rest of the characters of *The Tempest,* with the exception of Caliban and Ariel. These speeches are then followed by comments from Antonio addressed to Prospero.

Antonio, Prospero's brother, opens this second part with a brief speech which is in direct opposition to Prospero's. As we saw in Prospero's speech to Ariel, Prospero's great desire was to begin the quest, the journey towards self-knowledge, taking "The silent passage

[8] As Auden says (*The Dyer's Hand,* p. 104), "It is impossible consciously to approach a mirror without composing or 'making' a special face, and if we catch sight of our reflection unawares we rarely recognize ourselves. I cannot read my face in the mirror because I am already obvious to myself."

31

/ Into discomfort." In order to begin his journey, Prospero realized the necessity of putting aside the arts of illusion, chief among which is the belief that "the way of truth" is a way of communication, that it is possible to talk about "the smiling / Secret." Prospero is an intelligent man and, as such, tried throughout his life to find some escape from the problem of facing life. His escapes ranged from that of an "affectionate chat" to "saying something ironic or funny / On suffering." But none of these salved his anxiety, and since Ariel, the "Unanxious one," could offer no other solutions, Prospero was forced to come face to face with silence, to begin his journey in the situation Auden places him—alone with himself. There is a vast difference between Prospero's "I am that I am" and Antonio's "I am I, Antonio, / By choice myself alone." Antonio, filled with malice, considers himself the true "isolatoe," the man who stands alone, satirically viewing the surrounding world. Yet his "aloneness" is not really aloneness at all, it is a pose constructed for Prospero's benefit, for Antonio can be himself alone only as long as Prospero is aware that Antonio is separate, only as long as Prospero feels the "need to love." But Prospero has reached the point where he feels no guilt for what happened between Antonio and himself. He tempted him, Antonio fell, but neither need be sorry, that is over, the books are balanced, there is no tension. He no longer feels the need to know Antonio.

Auden places Antonio's self-conscious selfishness in direct contrast to Prospero's desire for self-knowledge. One of the chief reasons for Prospero's change is his recognition of the separateness of human beings and of the impossibility of bridging the gap between them; however, he also recognizes that the belief that the universe is centered upon oneself is the height of delusion. Antonio, wrapped in his total egocentricity, completely misreads Prospero's desire. He feels that Prospero wishes, as does Antonio himself, to become a child and enter "The green occluded pasture." This is a total reversal of Prospero's quest, an escape from self-knowledge rather than a move in its direction. Prospero saw himself as a child, "a sobbing dwarf" torn with hatred for the "giants" above him and filled with a desire to escape "a father's imperfect justice." Antonio, however, obviously feels that childhood is the perfect time for fulfillment of the ego, the time of innocent egocentricity. Since this is what he wants, he assumes that it is also what Prospero most desires.

By making Antonio and Prospero opposite numbers, Auden makes a definite value judgment on the validity of the stances of the two men and, indirectly, helps to clarify what he feels the difference between art and life really means. Prospero was an artist, a genuine one, using his art to manipulate the stuff of life and, by manipulation, helping himself to avoid a confrontation with reality, the meaning of life. His casting aside of his art is an attempt to be honest, to face life with no power but his own open ignorance. This, to Auden, is of extreme importance.

In the 1930s Auden felt that art was perhaps the key to the improvement of man and his world. Like Shelley, he viewed the poet as a secular priest, leading his flock out of error into truth. But by the 1940s, although the would-be leader/priest still struggled through his poems, his voice had gone sour to Auden. The secular leader had become manifest in Hitler and Auden's hope had turned to horror. Thus the didactic power of art which Auden had praised in the thirties became that of the very Devil himself, and the way to truth became the path to error.

Viewed in this way, the artist then becomes, if not evil, at very best a poseur, believing he has that which he has not. From the view of the artist as the possible savior we have the reverse image; Ariel looks in the mirror and sees Caliban. So, when Prospero puts down his magic cloak, Antonio picks it up. But, instead of being the writer, the creator behind the work, Antonio is the cheapest type of artist, the actor who has gone mad and believes he is his role.

In Prospero and Antonio, then, we have two versions of the artist: Prospero, the one-time artist who has begun to recognize the true value of both his art and himself, setting out on his silent quest for truth; and Antonio, the would-be artist, but in a totally negative sense, dependent upon the attention of others to save him from really seeing himself.

This is the first of many reversals Auden effects in the long works of the forties, trying to rid himself of his old ideas and find a poetic voice for his new ones. Here his method is art and artist as metaphor for life and living in an attempt to correct his errors of the thirties. In the next character to appear, Ferdinand, we are given Auden's new view of lyric, romantic love, the belief that only with another can man find "The Right Required Time, The Real Right Place." For Ferdinand, as Prospero says, "today it all looks so easy." Auden sees no evil in this naïveté, only the danger of what might come once it has worn off. He is concerned for Ferdinand and Miranda when the newness of being loved is gone and the necessity of loving sets in. For, when the loved one is familiar, it is much more difficult to consider him or her "beloved."

The Sea and the Mirror gives the audience a new perspective on the familiar characters of *The Tempest.* The play's action has concluded, the situations which brought drama to the relationships between the characters have been resolved. The characters are left static in time and space—alone or in groups. Like the figures on Keats' Grecian Urn, they cannot move. Auden makes them talk about the only thing they have left: themselves. They are isolated in their own backyards. And we, as audience, see them as individuals outside of action, separated from the tensions of a "situation." Since the Stage Manager has prepared us, we expect them to deal with themselves as selves, to discuss with us the difference between what we feel them to be (what they "seem"), and what they are.

The elimination of dramatic situation, which marks the major difference between *The Tempest* and *The Sea and the Mirror*, does not mean that the latter is not dramatic. What has happened is that Auden has effected a shift in dramatic emphasis. In place of the character conflict of *The Tempest*, Auden substitutes a conflict of ideas. When *The Tempest* concludes, the dukedom is recovered, the lovers are brought together, the sinners are forgiven, and they all live happily ever after. But, Auden asks, do they? Will they? What if this were life instead of art? What if the characters—like living beings—had to wake up the next morning with the performance in the past?

Auden makes them do just that. When the Stage Manager appears in front of the curtain, he makes sure that the audience knows that "these revels now are ended," and thus brings the characters of art into the world of life. He brings the mirror and the sea together. The internal conflict between the audience and the characters is substituted for the external conflict of character against character. We (the audience) see the characters as humans like ourselves, and yet, in a way, we still feel protected because we know more about them than they do about us. We expect answers from them, but we—as Critics—do not feel obliged to give answers ourselves. We have become, in effect, the mirror, from which no answer is expected.

Auden so structures *The Sea and the Mirror* that we see the characters as representing all aspects of the human spectrum in their reactions to the problems of living and dying. For instance, Prospero and Antonio represent extremes in man's concern with the self, while Ferdinand represents the idealized romantic concern for another.

Stephano, the drunken butler and the next character

to appear, directs his remarks to his belly ("Embrace me, belly, like a bride"). He shows by his words, and by what he does not say, that he is a man who has given himself up without battle. His speech is filled with the drunkard's images of family. His escape from reality is found in his appetites, represented physically by his belly. Beginning as "Dear daughter," the product of the man, it has become, through a diet of "humble pie and swallowed pride," the mother or "Wise nanny," behind whose "skirts your son must hide."

What Stephano has tried to do throughout his life is to reach "The green occluded pasture as a child"—the pasture that Antonio supposed Prospero desired to reach; he has sought relief from anxiety by trying to blindfold himself to it. And this he realizes. He knows that the problem is one of responsible identity (this is the reason for the recurrent family imagery in his speech; the parent must take responsibility for the child), and in his confusion of family roles he goes so far as to ask straight out, "Child? Mother?" He recognizes the "need for pardon," but he has not put himself in a position to receive pardon. His self-pity, although not as offensive as Antonio's arrogance, is just as deadly. And, as he ends his speech with the line which concludes each of his previous stanzas, "A lost thing looks for a lost name," we find no resolution, no arrogance, merely self-pitying resignation.

Gonzalo, the "aged councillor," speaks next. Like Alonso who is to follow him, Gonzalo is a variation on the Prospero–Antonio reaction of age to the preparation for death. Although not defiant as Antonio is, he is still not prepared to quest with Prospero. He feels his life has ended. Yet it has not ended, and Antonio is very nearly correct when he refers to him as "Decayed Gonzalo" (Gonzalo refers to himself as "rusting flesh"). He is filled with regret, but at the same time he is able to say that "There is nothing to forgive." He brings together "the Absurd" and "The Already There" through the device of a "storm's decision." And he turns Prospero's voyage, "Sailing alone, out over seventy fathoms," into the idea of aging human flesh idly waiting. With Gonzalo, Prospero's activity becomes passivity, and the quest for self-knowledge becomes resignation to the caprice of "the Absurd."

Alonso, like Gonzalo, is old and is ready to step aside, "now ready to welcome / Death. . . ." But, unlike "Decayed Gonzalo," he is

> . . . rejoicing in a new love,
> A new peace, having heard the solemn
> Music strike and seen the statue move
> To forgive our illusion.

He feels himself at peace in the garden. Here the contrast between Alonso and Gonzalo becomes quite clear. Gonzalo felt that "There is nothing to forgive," while Alonso feels that in order to find peace our illusion must be forgiven. Gonzalo turned to the imagery of science, with his emphasis on "The storm's decision" and his boyhood learning of "a formula," while Alonso chooses art, with the music striking and the statue moving. We are back with the Stage Manager's two unreliable alternatives set forth in the "Preface"—one, science, laying hands on us, and the other, art, moving before our senses. Alonso, although not "decaying," is "dying Alonso." He is reaching for a peace that comes too easily, from a pattern that is too simple.

But the advice which Alonso offers to his son is, despite the pompous tone, a map for what Auden considers the quest through the symbolic landscape of the soul. All of the dominant images of *The Sea and the Mirror*—in fact, of most of Auden's poetry of the forties —appear in this letter, and it merits close scrutiny.

Alonso begins with a caution to his son, the would-be king, to "Ascend your throne majestically" but to beware of the sea of too little consciousness ("the waters where fish / See sceptres descending with no wish / To touch them"), and the desert of too much consciousness ("the sands where a crown / Has the status of a broken-down / Sofa or mutilated status . . .").[9] This desert ("The sunburnt superficial kingdom") and this sea ("The cold deep") are the two poles in Auden's conception of possible living human hells—between them stretches "The Way of Justice," a tightrope like the one on which "the nonchalant couple" waltzed in the opening stanza of the poem. But waltzing is prohibited here because there can be no nonchalance; the dangers of falling are too carefully spelled out. Both the sea and the desert offer an escape into illusion, an illusion of permanence, because when a person inhabits one or the other, there is no hint that the opposite exists —after all, one can always refuse to look into the mirror. But Alonso counsels his son to look into himself, for only by doing so can man discover what he really is, without the ornaments and trappings of what he feels to be his world.

Once man is able to examine himself as he is, Alonso says, he will begin to doubt the permanence of any position in "this world of face," and will begin to see life as it is, firmly locked in time, with dangers in every moment. The chief danger is, of course, what Alonso calls "our illusion." This illusion is man's belief (and this is particularly true in the case of prince, leader, hero, or artist) that he can control his circumstances, that he can order the world around him, that he is able —by himself alone—to bring meaning and direction to life. Man must, in order to prevent this illusion,

> . . . Remember when
> Your climate seems a permanent home
> For marvellous creatures and great men,

[9] See Auden's assertion that "The sea . . . is the symbol of primitive potential power as contrasted with the desert of actualized triviality, of living barbarism versus lifeless decadence" (*The Enchaféd Flood* [New York: Random House, 1950], p. 20).

38

What griefs and convulsions startled Rome,
Ecbatana, Babylon.

The "climate" is the temper of each man's life, and each
man carries his own "Rome, / Ecbatana, Babylon." If
man falls, as each man does, Alonso's advice is quite
simple: "Believe your pain."

This is the second step towards salvation in Alonso's
(and Auden's) terms. It is also an almost direct echo of
what Job was asked to do. When one has examined
himself honestly and discovered his own insignificance
when confronted by the universe, he has no choice
(save suicide) but to believe his pain and, from believing, to praise its cause. This is where Alonso differs
most radically from Gonzalo, for Gonzalo's final position is passive, one of waiting for "The Already There"
to lay hands upon him, while Alonso's is active, one of
praising "the Absurd." The act of faith is translated, for
Alonso, into applause for the performance—however
shoddy—because it is there.

Sebastian's sestina, which follows a short, sad sailors'
song by the Master and the Boatswain, is composed
about the words "dream," "sword," "day," "alive,"
"proof," "crown." The basic opposition is day/dream,
proof/alive, and sword/crown, but these words work
against each other throughout the poem, giving, by
their interaction, Sebastian's position in relation to the
ideas of *The Sea and the Mirror* as a whole.

As Sebastian begins, his "dream / Where Prudence
flirted with a naked sword" has crumbled: "It is day."
And as he wakes, he sees that his dream was just that—
illusion: "Nothing has happened; we are still alive,"
and he is Sebastian, "wicked still" but with his "proof /
Of mercy," the fact that he is "without a crown."

He sees now, as evidenced in the second stanza, that
his dream had begun in a children's day ruled by
wishes ("all wishes wear a crown / And anything pretended is alive") and that his error—although it was

not his fault, precipitated as it was by the sadness of beginning to awake to a world where there is a distinct difference between the possible and the impossible— was to plunge still further "into that dream."

In Sebastian's own imaginary kingdom each child rules, and the sadness which signals "to our children's day" is the dawning of the realization that this is not the case in life. It was impossible for Sebastian to accept this sadness; for he felt, as Antonio still does, that he could force his will upon the world and make it obey. What he sees now is that forcing his childish ego upon the world is listening to "the lie of Nothing."

He realizes that the world in which we live is one which we cannot control, but it is one in which we are alive. And he is ready to accept the fact. This world which Sebastian calls "Right Here" is not Ferdinand's "Real Right Place," but it exists nonetheless. It is not necessarily a happy place, but that is as it should be; Sebastian smiles *because* he trembles.

Trinculo, the clown, appears next and offers a portrait of the artist—the artist caught by his art and whatever it is that lies behind it. He refers to himself as a "cold clown" who warms "Mechanic, merchant, king" from a "solitude / Undreamed of by their fat." But he has no ability to warm himself.

He is man dehumanized, the artist depersonalized, from whom "A flock of words fly out" when "A terror shakes my tree." The artistic process here is purely mechanical—the artist is shaken by fear into speech which in turn produces laughter. Yet, Trinculo perceives something behind the fear, he realizes that it is not merely chance. For the "wild images" which are both cause and substance of his work come "Out of *your* freezing sky" (italics mine) with what seems to him to be a personal message:

> That I . . .
> May get my joke and die.

Trinculo realizes that his "joke" is on man and about man's mortality, and that the "terror" shaking his tree (which he turns into laughter) comes from a "you" as opposed to his "I." This is what Antonio refers to later in the poem when he says, "My humour is my own," for he knows that for him there is no universal joke, or so he would have Prospero believe.

The second major section of *The Sea and the Mirror* concludes with a villanelle delivered by Miranda. It echoes, in a sense, Ferdinand's earlier speech and also, in its youthful naïveté adds a view into Miranda's character. It is a fairy-story recapitulation of her life, with Caliban ("the Black Man"), Sycorax ("The Witch"), Prospero ("The Ancient"), and Ferdinand ("My Dear One") all appearing in fairy-tale disguises. It also is an attempt, in her naïveté, to bring together the worlds of sea and mirror in the permanence of love. She says:

> My Dear One is mine as mirrors are lonely,
> As the poor and sad are real to the good king,
> And the high green hill sits always by the sea.

The most complex of these analogies is ". . . as mirrors are lonely." Since the function of the mirror is to give an image, when no one is looking into the mirror, its function is destroyed. A "lonely" mirror would be that which reflects no face, as Miranda or her "Dear One" each would be without the other. But, of course, mirrors are not lonely, no matter how nice it may be to think so; mirrors are no more lonely than lovers are eternally true. After what has occurred in *The Sea and the Mirror*, Miranda's naïveté becomes all the more clear and her speech seems almost ironic. We can hope that Ferdinand will be "the good king," but we are aware of so many evil or weak ones that we cannot help but smile. Time is the element of which Miranda is unaware; her love and Ferdinand's goodness seem as permanent to her as "The high green hill . . . by the sea." In a way, of course, they are, for the sea and time will work upon the hill in such a manner that it will *not* sit "always by the sea."

Once the basic analogies and images are established, Miranda begins her fairy-story autobiography and ends with Ferdinand kissing her awake. She says that "no one was sorry," but in order "to remember our changing garden" it is necessary to be "linked as children in a circle dancing." Here Miranda is correct. In order to remember the Garden of Innocence, the permanence of illusion, it is necessary to be "linked as children." The child, as we have seen before in *The Sea and the Mirror*, believes in the world, in its permanence, and in his control over it. The circle is for Auden the place out of time. By linking childish hands, Miranda thinks it is possible to have forever, innocently, the "Dear One" or "Dear Other." This is the illusion of the naïve, and it is Miranda's.

Caliban's speech, which stands as part three of *The Sea and the Mirror*, is divided into four major sections. The first section is addressed to Shakespeare, the second to a would-be poet in the audience, and the third to the audience as a whole. In the fourth, Caliban speaks for himself, the other characters, and the audience.

It is by far the largest part of *The Sea and the Mirror* and is in many ways the most complicated. Auden means to have Caliban and Ariel represent two aspects of man's nature, not two men.[10] All the other charac-

[10] As Auden says (*The Dyer's Hand*, pp. 132–133): "Over against Caliban, the embodiment of the natural, stands the invisible spirit of imagination, Ariel. (In a stage production, Caliban should be as monstrously conspicuous as possible, and, indeed, suggest, as far as decency permits, the phallic. Ariel, on the other hand, except when he assumes a specific disguise at Prospero's order, e.g., when he appears as a harpy, should, ideally, be invisible, a disembodied voice, an ideal which, in these days of microphones and loudspeakers, should be realizable.)"

ters of *The Sea and the Mirror* are humans, caught in life with its inherent anxiety, but Caliban and Ariel seem to be outside of it, representing, respectively, the sea and the mirror. Caliban has no identity because he is caught up totally within himself as a functioning animal; he is, as Auden elsewhere terms the sea, "that state of barbaric vagueness and disorder." [11] Caliban is engaged, as (so Auden says) is man, in trying to pull himself into existence. Ariel, on the other hand, is past human experience: he is the mirror, "lonely as mirrors are lonely"; he cannot say "I" because he does not have an "I."

Auden's use of Ariel's inhumanity is quite simple; and the equation of Ariel with the mirror or, in a more philosophical sense, with man pushed beyond humanity, is quite clear. Auden's use of Caliban is much more complicated, for Caliban seems to become, like Don Quixote, something more than his creator intended. One can no more than guess why Auden chose to change Caliban from the earthy opposite of Ariel to the proponent of the final philosophical position of *The Sea and the Mirror*, but one can trace, with some accuracy, the process of this change.

After a brief introduction, Caliban begins his speech in the guise of the audience complaining to Shakespeare about Caliban's presence in *The Tempest*. He says that the audience expects illusion from the theater, a "world of faery," that beyond the proscenium is a "world of freedom without anxiety, sincerity without loss of vigour, feeling that loosens rather than ties the tongue. . . ." This is a world that the audience has neither the desire nor the expectation to enter. It is a pretty world, capable of resolution, a far cry from reality. The world of art enjoys "an infinitely indicative mood, an eternally present tense, a limitlessly active voice," while the "shambling slovenly makeshift world" of reality must go on within time, without resolution.

[11] *The Enchaféd Flood*, p. 7.

Art is pattern; life is without pattern. In fact, on the artistic "far side of the mirror the general will to compose, to form at all costs a felicitous pattern becomes the *necessary cause* of any particular effort to live," while on the real side of the mirror "it is . . . *accidental effect.*"

What Caliban, speaking for the audience, expresses is the audience's desire not to see itself in the world of art. Because, in seeing itself there, it would see itself grotesqued, as Caliban is grotesqued. There is no resolution for Caliban in the world of art, because he is a misfit as the audience would be were it to find itself transported to the stage. Caliban claims that the audience sees itself as he is: embarrassed and embarrassing.

Auden begins his development of the character of Caliban with this premise. Caliban is a misfit on the stage because he is too different from anyone else in *The Tempest.* There is no one with whom he can reconcile himself, no one to forgive him. He is as out of place there as Ariel, his opposite number, would be in the real world. As Caliban (for the audience) says, "We want no Ariel here, breaking down our picket fences in the name of fraternity, seducing our wives in the name of romance, and robbing us of our sacred pecuniary deposits in the name of justice."

This is the first picture of Caliban: the rejected, unresolved, "impervious disgrace" of Prospero. He is the opposite of Ariel, as the real world is the opposite of art. He is flesh as opposed to spirit, life as opposed to beyond-life. He differs from the "human" characters of *The Tempest* in that he is absolute, while they are composed of bits of him and of Ariel in varying proportions. There is, in short, nothing to be done with him.

Yet Ariel's opposite talks like a literary critic, and not only in his guise as audience and not merely in jest. He is cognizant—not a rough beast, but aware of himself and his position. Like the other characters of *The Tempest* whom Auden has used in *The Sea and the*

Mirror, Caliban has been brought "down stage with red faces and no applause"; he is as he is, not as Shakespeare created him but the man behind the creation. Caliban is the character whom Auden chooses to break down the invisible "fourth wall" because he is the character least fitted to the action of the play, and thus the character most likely to puzzle the audience and, probably, the one about whom they would most like to know more. So we see him, shaggy, rough, but speaking in a different voice, speaking as he wants to, according to choice. The effect is shocking at first, like seeing a friend who has changed totally overnight. Then it becomes comic, or charming, depending on one's sense of humor; but finally it becomes clear that what we are listening to is not Caliban locked in the world of art, but Caliban freed and returned to life. We have viewed the other characters from a certain, safe distance; we have been able to ask them questions and yet have remained free from any real danger ourselves. With the appearance of Caliban, this freedom is destroyed. He immediately takes our place as audience and asks questions for us, makes demands on the author and tells us what we really want to ask.

He then turns to an individual in the audience, calling him a would-be poet and placing him in competition with the author of *The Tempest.* He gives a catalogue of the artist's hopes and fears and, finally, confronts him with the worst fear of all: that Caliban is present in each man, artist or not.

He begins by telling the would-be artist that when he starts to write he will feel Ariel to be his friend, that his "ornate mirror" will show him his Ariel face—himself as he wishes he were. But as he grows older and feels his creative powers weaken, he will become angry and frustrated by Ariel's presence and finally, saying "you are free," will stride up to Ariel only to

. . . stop dead, transfixed with horror at seeing reflected there, not what you had always expected to see, a conqueror smiling at a conqueror, both promising mountains and marvels, but a gibbering fist-clenched creature with which you are all too unfamiliar, for this is the first time indeed that you have met the only subject that you have, who is not a dream amenable to magic but the all too solid flesh you must acknowledge as your own. . . .

Caliban is, in short, man as he is, not as he would wish to be. Taking a poet for his example, Caliban points out that, in spite of his urge to find the perfection of spirit in this life, man is always left with one inescapable fact: his own flesh.

Caliban describes the poet's progress through life as an attempt to escape from life while deluding himself into thinking that he is not only facing life but ennobling it. As Caliban presents him, the poet is an everyday, ordinary, polite man. He has avoided the extremes of the martyr and the debauchee. He has spent his life avoiding pitfalls, aiming at what he considered the creative life, the moderate life. As a poet, he has lived the life that Alonso recommends to Ferdinand, a life in "the temperate city," allowing—as Caliban has him say—his real, temporal self "to do everything, in reason, that you liked." But this, for Caliban, has been no life at all: "Even deliberate ill-treatment would have been less unkind." Had the poet tried one extreme or the other, had he tried, like an ascetic, to purge the here and now, the flesh, or had he succumbed, like the debauchee, to a life of sensual satiety, the chances for all three of them— the poet, Caliban, and Ariel—to have arrived at the truth would have been greatly increased. Had the poet let himself go, he might have become one of "the best and worst of us" about whom Auden talks in "In Praise of Limestone." [12] As it is, the poet is neither one thing nor the other. He thought that he was in the arms of Ariel and so neglected Caliban; but he never hon-

[12] W. H. Auden, *Nones* (New York: Random House, 1951), p. 14.

estly faced either one of them and consequently never faced himself. He thought of his neglect of the here and now as his "exile" and now considers his life (as Caliban terms it, "the pains you never took with me") as "all lost."

Caliban is telling the poet that because of the poet's delusion (convincing himself that he was choosing Ariel when actually he was in a sort of limbo between Ariel and Caliban), he now is faced with his life without his talent. He is faced with living with the self he never really wanted but did not know how to get rid of, while the self he always wanted (and, in fact, thought was his) now mocks him by its absence.[13] The man who would have been the hero, the exceptional man, the man who thought he was a poet turns out to be merely a heretic.

Here, once again, is Auden's judgment on his own prior position. Prospero, Antonio, Trinculo, and now the unnamed would-be Shakespeare in the audience are all variants on a single theme. There can be no doubt that even here, in *The Sea and the Mirror*, Auden's feelings about his beliefs of the thirties amount to much more than mere chagrin. He knows that he was wrong. To him, the artist who believes he is more than a comedian is dangerously deluded if not consciously evil; he must remember he is playing a game which, if taken seriously, can only lead to personal and social moral chaos.

The last section of Caliban's speech is directed to the audience as a group, "you assorted, consorted speci-

[13] In "Jacob and the Angel" (a review of *Behold This Dreamer* by Walter de la Mare), *The New Republic*, December 27, 1939, p. 293, Auden goes into the problem in some detail. He says: ". . . for the night brings forth the day, the unconscious IT fashions the conscious fore-brain; the historical epoch grows the idea; the subject matter creates the technique—but it does so precisely in order that it may itself escape the bonds of the determined and the natural. The daemon creates Jacob the prudent Ego, not for the latter to lead, in self-isolation and contempt, a frozen attic life of its own, but to be a loving and reverent antagonist. . . ."

mens of the general popular type," and here he claims to be speaking for both Ariel and himself. He makes no attempt to answer our questions directly, for, as he says, "the mere fact that you have been able so anxiously to put them is in itself sufficient proof that you possess their answers."

The key word here is "anxiously." It is anxiety that is at the heart of the dramatic situation of Caliban's speech, as it is at the heart of *The Sea and the Mirror* as a whole. In the Stage Manager's "Preface" questions were posed which set the scene for the speeches to follow. These unanswerable and rhetorical questions established the function of the audience as participant, which is what keeps *The Sea and the Mirror* from being a "mere" commentary on *The Tempest*. The Stage Manager posed questions that brought about, or played upon, the anxiety of the audience. The characters' speeches which followed showed various human attitudes as possible answers. We, as audience, felt a certain safety, or found a balance to anxiety, in being able to hear answers without having to formulate them ourselves. But now Caliban moves downstage and says: ". . . at last it is you. . . ."

It is we who have moved out of "the childish spell" and into "the larger colder emptier room on this side of the mirror." It is we, whether as audience or reader, who are suddenly asked to make a choice when confronted with "the irreconcilable differences between . . . Caliban's reiterated affirmation of what . . . furnished circumstances categorically are, and . . . Ariel's successive propositions as to everything else which they conditionally might be." In other words, we are pulled from the anxiety of viewer into the anxiety of participant.[14] We are asked to face the difference between

[14] Auden, in "Tradition and Value" (a review of *The Novel and the Modern World* by David Daitches), *The New Republic*, January 15, 1940, p. 90, says: "I welcome the atomization of society and I look forward to a socialism based on it, to the day when the disintegration of tradition will be as final and universal for the masses

what might be and what is, the "lion's mouth," between illusion and reality. And, not only are we asked to face this difference, we are asked to choose between two alternatives. As Caliban says, "you have . . . taken your first step."

This first step is recognizing that there is a difference between what is and what might be, and that we are forced to choose between them.[15] It is also recognizing that if we choose what is, what might be, in a worldly sense, is gone forever. Or, if we choose what might be, we lose what is. What do we do?

Caliban cautions that this is only the beginning of "The Journey of Life," that we have only reached "the Grandly Average Place," where we may, for the moment at least, find some small relief from anxiety. Ours is a "land of habit," of "stagestruck hope," but the land to which we are going, wherever it may be, will be "foreign, uncomfortable, and despotic."

Now we, as reader or audience, are placed in the position of so many of Auden's characters: at the beginning of the quest. Caliban—at least at this stage of his development—is not a questor; he merely personifies one possible choice. Instead of joining with us, he only cautions us not to engage either Ariel or himself as guides, not to choose either extreme, not to fall into either hell. Echoing Alonso, he asks each of us to try to make his own individual lonely way.

If we choose either Ariel or Caliban, we refute the

as it is already for the artist, because it will be only when they fully realize their 'aloneness' and accept it, that men will be able to achieve a real unity through common recognition of their diversity. . . ."

[15] Auden says (*The Dyer's Hand*, p. 133) that: "Imagination is beyond good *and* evil. Without imagination I remain an innocent animal, unable to become anything but what I already am. In order to become what I should become, therefore, I have to put my imagination to work, and limit its playful activity to imagining those possibilities which, for me, are both permissible and real; if I allow it to be the master and play exactly as it likes, then I shall remain in a dreamlike state of imagining everything I might become, without getting round to ever becoming anything."

entire idea of the quest, because we will be asking for what might be rather than what is, we will be choosing illusion over reality. If we ask Caliban to

> . . . take us home with you, strong and swelling One, home to your promiscuous pasture where the minotaur of authority is just a roly-poly ruminant and nothing is at stake, those purring sites and amusing vistas . . . ,

he will take us instead to a county where,

> Cones from extinct volcanoes rise up abruptly from the lava plateau fissured by chasms and pitted with hot springs from which steam arises without interruption straight up into the windless rarified atmosphere.

Or, if we ask Ariel for

> . . . that Heaven of the Really General Case, where, tortured no longer by three dimensions and immune from temporal vertigo, Life turns into Light, absorbed for good into the permanently stationary, completely self-sufficient, absolutely reasonable One,

we will get instead

> . . . a night-mare which has all the wealth of exciting action and all the emotional poverty of an adventure story for boys, a state of perpetual emergency and everlasting improvisation where all is need and change.

Whether we choose the "facile, glad-handed highway" or "the virtuous averted track," we arrive at the same "abruptly dreadful end." Either way we are damned because we have tried to avoid the initial choice. We have asked for what we think we want and deserve, and, like the poet who thought he was choosing Ariel and ended up with Caliban, we have received precisely that which we do not want.

With a shrug of resignation and a hope "that I have had the futile honour of addressing the blind and the deaf," Caliban moves from a discussion of the audience's fate to a discussion of his own. He compares his condition to "the serio-comic embarrassment of the dedicated dramatist, who, in representing to you your condition of estrangement from the truth, is doomed to fail the more he succeeds."

This is the turning point in the character of Caliban as it is the turning point in *The Sea and the Mirror*. What Caliban says is that the more clearly he sees "the truth," the less able he is to articulate it, and that the closer he comes to articulating "truth," the further he gets from our "condition." Moreover, even if he is able to articulate both the "truth" and our "condition of estrangement," he must indicate that there is a way to proceed from one to the other even if he is only able to say that "an awareness of the gap is in itself a bridge." An impasse. Where the sea and the mirror meet is on the ground of the dramatist.

By using Caliban's notion of himself as a dramatist, Auden is attempting to explain his use of art versus reality as a metaphor for illusion versus reality in life. The problem posed by the characters in *The Sea and the Mirror* is how one gets off the stage of life, and into what—if anything—is real beyond it.

By this time Caliban is ready to bring the cast out and the audience up, to join "down stage with red faces and no applause." No longer are we audience, actors, characters, or representatives of abstract psychological forces. We all stand together to listen to Caliban. He says: "There is nothing to say. There never has been. . . . There is no way out. There never was."

Now the "I," the "you," the "he," "she," and "it" have been brought together and forced into a "we," and "we" seem no further along than we were when the Stage Manager left us together at the beginning. Indeed, we seem to have regressed, for there is a new audience now: "that Wholly Other Life from which we are separated by an essential emphatic gulf. . . ." And we, actors, Stage Manager, Critics, and audience, have given a bad show; ". . . there was not a single aspect of our whole production . . . for which a kind word could, however patronisingly, be said."

This, of course, is precisely the point towards which Auden has been working in *The Sea and the Mirror*. It is when we realize that our life bears the same relation to "that Wholly Other Life" that a stage production bears to our life that we can glimpse the possibility of perfection. It is "Not that we have improved. . . ." All the evils and inadequacies of life are still present, perhaps even worse. "Only now it is not in spite of them but with them that we are blessed. . . ." It is because we are anxious that we know there is an "unbothered state," because we are isolated that there is a "restored relation."

Caliban has ceased to be an abstract quality and has ceased to be an advisor. He now stands, as he claims we felt him to be standing all along, among us. He speaks for us as our priest using the "we" and directing us towards a "he." His speech is an attempt, by will, to believe; to relieve anxiety by believing in it. The questions posed by the Stage Manager are answered with no answer. We are asked to believe that "it is just here, among the ruins and the bones, that we may rejoice in the perfected Work which is not ours."

It seems a fine ending: Caliban, arms upraised; actors and audience, heads bowed; all praising "the Absurd." But Auden does not choose to end it there. He chooses, rather, what might be called a "dying fall." In the "Postscript," a song offered by Ariel to Caliban with the aid of an echo from the Prompter, Auden reintroduces the "I."

Ariel's song is based upon the "you-I" opposition he shared with Caliban. Ariel represents what might be as opposed to what is: a "Fleet, persistent shadow cast / By your lameness. . . ." If man accepts what is (his "lameness"), he will stop chasing that which might be (the "shadow"). Ariel can only "sing as you [Caliban] reply." And for Ariel the reply must be "I." Unless Caliban (or man—for now Caliban is one of us) holds onto his ego—his necessity to say "I"—there can be no "you" for Ariel. Ariel exists only in opposition to Caliban. If Caliban chooses to see himself and his life as illusion, and thus eliminate the opposition, there is no place for Ariel to go.

When Ariel says, "only / As I am can I / Love you as you are," he is begging his opposite not to face humanity, but to remain below it, to remain "the Sea," as Ariel himself remains "the Mirror." He wants Caliban to be "ill" for Ariel's "health," to be "lonely" for Ariel's "company," to "cry" so that Ariel may "sing."

But at the end of each stanza, there is no reply from Caliban. The Prompter prompts "I," but there is no response from Caliban and the "I" from the Prompter seems to run into Ariel's next line, as though the Prompter were prompting Ariel. This effect lends a desperation to Ariel's speech, and when Ariel closes with his prediction of "What we shall become, / One evaporating sigh," the Prompter's "I" ends *The Sea and the Mirror* on a plaintive, futile note, not at all the note of "restored relation" prophesied by Caliban at the end of his speech. This is because what Ariel is asking for is a maintenance of the status quo in his relationship to Caliban; he wants to maintain "I" in relation to "you," while Caliban has already gone from this to the "we" in relation to "he."

So Ariel is left alone, terrified that with the loss of

Caliban has come a loss of self. The "Unanxious one"—left with no one to sing to—has become anxious. The others, from Caliban to the other characters to the audience, have become a "we" looking towards "that Wholly Other Life"; the actors are no longer characters but living human beings. Only Ariel remains in character, wearing costume and makeup—only Ariel is "A lost thing looking for a lost name."

The Sea and the Mirror is quite an achievement, but where does Auden stand in all this? Which voice is his? Is it Caliban's? Prospero's? Alonso's? My guess is all and none. In using an (at least) semidramatic form in *The Sea and the Mirror,* Auden gives himself freedom to experiment with personifications of various viewpoints without being forced to choose any one mask as his own.

Prospero, for instance, is at least partially right, for he recognizes the essential loneliness of any spiritual journey. Yet he seems too Kierkegaardian to be completely representative of Auden's thought. While he is "Sailing alone, out over seventy thousand fathoms," one still sees those "Ironic points of light" of "September 1, 1939" and cannot help feeling that Prospero does not.

Alonso, too, is unsatisfactory. Although he seems to know the way and the many pitfalls along it, he is abstracted. Welcoming death, he leaves life before his time and makes his last years, days, or hours meaningless.

Perhaps Caliban comes closest of all to being Auden's voice. He is a priest, at least at the last stage of his development, and we know that the preacher was a favorite guise of the earlier Auden. He brings us together, joins with us, and tells us we are blessed not in spite of but with our failings. He knows the right way and the proper attitude to approach "that Wholly Other Life." Still, there is something wrong with Caliban, something of the cold fish about him that is much closer to Malin of *The Age of Anxiety* than to the persona of "Horae

54

Canonicae." We cannot help but feel, somehow, that Ariel should be with us.

The elimination of voices should not be considered in any way accidental. One of the chief objections to *The Sea and the Mirror* is that one cannot find Auden in it. One cannot, and, in a sense, one should not try. I do not mean that one should not examine the various characters and test their voices against what one imagines Auden's to be. In fact, that is precisely what I have done in this chapter. What one should not do is make a final assignation of character to author. None of the voices in *The Sea and the Mirror* is Auden's because to him they are all, in varying degrees, false. It is easy to see Auden's dismissal of the artist in the inept malignity of Antonio or the fears of Trinculo, but one must also be careful to notice the inability of Auden to accept Prospero's particular brand of "aloneness" or Alonso's resignation; and, in Caliban, the good but ineffectual priest, to see a benign, preliminary study for the failure of Malin in *The Age of Anxiety*.

III

For The Time Being

For the Time Being, the companion piece to *The Sea and the Mirror* and the title piece of the 1944 volume, is an attempt on Auden's part to write an oratorio. Not nearly so dazzling either in technique or idea as its companion piece, it is nonetheless a complex and puzzling work. And although it was written before *The Sea and the Mirror*, from 1941 to 1942, it would seem that Auden felt it to be an extension of the later work.

As we have seen in *The Sea and the Mirror*, Auden likes to begin with the setting, letting us know where we are. In *The Sea and the Mirror* Auden placed us in a theater; the performance is over, and we are dissatisfied. In *For the Time Being*, he places us in our own living rooms. Waiting, dulled, tired, we check the time, but "The clock on the mantelpiece / Has nothing to recommend." Nor do our mirrors, for "the face in the glass" does not "Appear nobler than our own." We are alone, staring, "As darkness and snow descend / On all personality." There is no passion in anger or love—our leader, "Portly Caesar yawns." Auden seems to be approximating the situation which Eliot presents in the "The Waste Land" before the advent of "the cruellest month." Yet there is grave danger in this appearance of passivity. The shuffling, mumbling, and yawning are not gestures of the droning status quo; they represent to Auden the slip over the edge of nothingness. Negation permeates the entire stanza. The "darkness and snow" seem to be carrying us, as they descend, into a final night where things, attitudes, indeed life itself are "nothing," "nor," "not," and the sense of Portly Caesar's "I know" seems to be more *no* than *know*. Even the sound of the word "snow" (particularly in the last two lines of the stanza) underlines the negation (s-no). The entire stanza sounds more like an end than a beginning.

It is winter: real winter, since it is the Christmas season; symbolic winter, since we are dulled, cold, or apathetic in the face of the negation of the "darkness and snow." We are placed in juxtaposition with the ancient world on the eve of the birth of Christ. Yet we are very much locked in the present, in "the Time Being." [1]

In the first chorus, then, Auden establishes the setting. In the first semichorus, he makes his first comment and asks his first question:

> Can great Hercules keep his
> Extraordinary promise
> To reinvigorate the Empire?

He also answers it, for Hercules, the superhero of the ancient world, is

> Utterly lost, he cannot
> Even locate his task but
> Stands in some decaying orchard
> . . . .
> Seeing no one at all. . . .

The Sea and the Mirror also opened with a posing of questions, yet they were deliberately unanswerable; they were meant to puzzle both reader and character

[1] As Auden says in "Augustus to Augustine" (a review of *Christianity and Classical Culture* by Charles N. Cochrane), *The New Republic*, September 25, 1944, pp. 374–376: "[Man] is to be neither an anarchist nor a non-political 'idiot,' but to act now, with an eye fixed, neither nostalgically on the past nor dreamily on some ideal future, but on eternity—'redeeming the time'—in the words of Sidney Smith, he is to 'trust in God and take short views.'"

and, by provoking reaction and response, to give action to *The Sea and the Mirror*. What man must learn from *The Sea and the Mirror* is that there is *no* solution for the "smiling / Secret"—or at least none that man can understand. He must accept his situation and praise God for the fact that He is not man.

But in *For the Time Being* all questions are answerable (save for the final one: What do we do "For the Time Being"?): "Will Hercules save us?" "No." "Who will?" "Christ." [2] *For the Time Being* is quite simply a celebration of the presence of God; *The Sea and the Mirror* a celebration of His mystery. *The Sea and the Mirror* is about man's searching for God; *For the Time Being* is about what man does when he sees Him.

At the opening of *For the Time Being*, Christ is not yet here. The other two choruses and one semichorus of the first section of Part I, "Advent," add to the scene and situation given in the first chorus and semichorus. Not only are the "darkness and snow" of winter descending, but with them comes the end of the ancient world as "Winter completes an age / With its thorough levelling." The Empire as man has known it will not be invigorated, and even the individual is lost, for "Ice condenses on the bone." Yet, man and his world are not merely freezing to death, for the winter brings fear and anxiety and "a wild passion / To destroy and be destroyed."

This "wild passion" is in each individual as he feels his secure "civil garden" begin to wither and die, and it brings on individual anxiety.[3] It is also a fear of "The

[2] In "Augustus to Augustine" Auden says (p. 374): ". . . to the classical apotheosis of the Man-God, Augustine opposes a Christian belief in Jesus Christ, the God-Man. The former is a Hercules who compels recognition by the great deeds he does in establishing for the common people the law, order and prosperity they cannot establish for themselves, by his manifestation of superior power; the latter reveals to fallen man that God is love by suffering, i.e., by refusing to compel recognition, choosing instead to be a victim of man's self-love."

[3] Auden says in "The Means of Grace" (a review of *The Nature and Destiny of Man* by Reinhold Niebuhr), *The New Republic*,

evil and armed," the external enemy who makes the weather smell of hate and "the houses smell of our fear." As his world collapses, man fears for his life and his soul.[4]

The picture presented in this first section of *For the Time Being* is a solemn one, both in subject and in tone, like the speech of the Stage Manager in *The Sea and the Mirror* before he breaks the mood with his "Well, who in his own backyard . . ." of the last stanza.[5] Much of the same ironic effect is achieved in *For the Time Being* by Auden's use of a conversational speech by the Narrator in the second section of "Advent." He begins by itemizing the disasters and fears of life, prefacing each with an "if" (for example, "If all sailings have been cancelled till further notice . . .") and concluding with, "That is not at all unusual for this time of year." He then says, "If that were all we should know how to manage." "If that were all." The point, of course, is that "that" is not all. The usual attitude of "taking the bad with the good" is no longer viable. The usual "pattern composed / By the ten thousand odd things that can possibly happen" is no longer "permanent in a general average way."

The Narrator is talking about the childlike state of innocence, of individual security when "to cut our losses / And bury our dead was really quite easy," and it was possible for men to say, "We are children of God." But, as he goes on to say, ". . . then we were children." The world that is gone at the beginning of *For the Time Being* is "The green occluded pasture." [6] The children's day of which Sebastian spoke, "where all

June 2, 1941, p. 766: ". . . the temptation to sin is what the psychologist calls anxiety, and the Christian calls lack of faith."

[4] Auden says in "Tract for the Times" (a review of *Christianity and Power Politics* by Reinhold Niebuhr), *The Nation*, January 4, 1941, p. 25: ". . . man cannot live without a sense of the Unconditional: if he does not consciously walk in fear of the Lord, then his unconscious sees to it that he has something else, airplanes or secret police, to walk in fear of."

[5] Auden, *Collected Poetry*, p. 352.

[6] *Ibid.*, p. 361.

wishes wear a crown," [7] is ended: "That was a moment ago." The Narrator is not speaking of death; indeed, "the world of space where events re-occur is still there." What brings on the despair and anxiety is that "now it's no longer real."

The "smiling / Secret" of the Stage Manager in *The Sea and the Mirror* is seen here as a glimpse of the reality of an eternity that is a "nowhere / Where time never moves and nothing can ever happen." Man's individual identity "has become a fiction," and what he now sees is that his "true existence / Is decided by no one and has no importance to love." Winter has revealed the limbo from which there is no escape, the void or, as the Narrator terms it, "the wrath of God."

This is the core of the individual anxiety expressed in the first two sections of "Advent" in *For the Time Being.* Life is not only terrible and filled with pain, but now it is no longer even real. Yet what *is* real? Nothing, it would seem. Life may be a merry-go-round out of control, but stopping it would mean spinning off into an abyss of silence.

What the Narrator, beginning with a conversational, almost ironic tone, has led us to is a dead end, senseless but nonetheless there, where, as the Chorus says, "Alone, Alone, about a dreadful wood / Of conscious evil runs a lost mankind." He has led us to the point where men (as Chorus) "who must die demand a miracle." [8] Mankind demands to know "Where is that Law for which we broke our own, / Where now that Justice?" Why has "The Pilgrim Way . . . led to the Abyss"? Man had dreaded the "Goodness" of God and is now afraid that it might not be good. The Law has

[7] *Ibid.,* p. 370.

[8] Auden, in "A Preface to Kierkegaard" (a review of *Either/Or* by Søren Kierkegaard, ed. and trans. Swenson and Lowrie), *The New Republic,* May 15, 1944, p. 683, says that the existential philosopher ". . . begins with man's immediate experience as a *subject,* i.e., as a being in *need,* an *interested* being whose life is at stake."

let him down because, instead of revelation, it has brought him to the abyss and he is unable to see across it to "that Wholly Other Life" or to realize, like Caliban, that "it is precisely in its negative image of judgement that we can positively envisage Mercy." [9] It is time for the "Wholly Other" to make a move.

There is a dirge-like quality to this chorus with its a-b-b-a-a rhyme scheme, and it is one of the most intense moments of *For the Time Being*. Through its intensity it heightens the calm, deliberate tone of the "Recitative" which follows. There is no attempt made in the "Recitative" to offer us a way out of the dilemma; it is merely a catalogue of the seemingly impossible conditions for the occurrence of the "miracle." It seems almost Kiplingesque in its list of *if's, as long as's, until's,* and *unless's*. Yet within the impossibility of the demands lies a description of man's condition in "the garden," and "the garden is the only place there is." Man must learn to live without feeling ("If the muscle can feel repugnance, there is still a false move to be made"); without hope for what might be ("If the mind can imagine tomorrow, there is still a defeat to remember"); without "accidental virtue" ("As long as there is an accidental virtue, there is a necessary vice"); and, above all, without self-consciousness ("As long as the self can say 'I,' it is impossible not to rebel"). In short, man is asked to relax, to be—as Gonzalo said in *The Sea and the Mirror*—"A simple locus now." [10] Man is asked to "see without looking, hear without listening, breathe without asking," and to believe that "The Real is what will strike you as really absurd." [11]

Following the agony of the Chorus, this catalogue itself seems absurd. It describes the unanxious state, the waiting in the garden, but gives us no help in getting

<hr>

[9] Auden, *Collected Poetry*, p. 402.
[10] *Ibid.*, p. 365.
[11] For a parallel description of the state of being in the garden, see Auden, "The Garden," *Collected Poetry*, p. 262.

there. In answer to the demand of the Chorus for a miracle, it replies, "You do not deserve one yet; when you stop asking, you will get one." It says to man at the nadir of anxiety: "Forget about yourself." But how does man stop asking questions? [12] For Job there was a voice from out of the whirlwind. But for the Chorus there is the matter-of-fact voice of a paternal, self-righteous-sounding priest, paraphrasing Kierkegaard.

It is no wonder, then, that the Chorus returns to questioning. Man does not stop inquiring until he is given in return either a question that he cannot possibly answer, or a fact that is incredible but undeniably real. The Chorus, having been given neither of these but only an idea of a "garden of Being that is only known in Existence / As the command to be never there," cannot but ask, "Oh where is that immortal and nameless Centre . . . ?"

The "Advent" section of *For the Time Being* closes with this questioning by the Chorus. The scene and situation are set. It is winter; life is lifeless; when man asks for reasons or help, he seems to get only riddles in reply. This is the dramatic conflict at the opening of *For the Time Being,* and the action of the work moves in two directions from this point: 1) inside man as an individual; 2) into the activity of the world outside. Auden uses this double movement in order to present the fact of the Incarnation and individual reactions to it.[13]

[12] Auden says elsewhere ("A Preface to Kierkegaard," p. 683): ". . . the basic human problem is man's anxiety in time; e.g., his present anxiety over himself in relation to his past and his parents (Freud), his present anxiety over himself in relation to his future and his neighbors (Marx), his present anxiety over himself in relation to eternity and God (Kierkegaard)."

[13] In "The Means of Grace," p. 765, Auden describes the importance of the Incarnation: "In the first place it asserts that at an actual moment in historical time, the Word was actually made Flesh, the possibility of the union of the finite with the infinite made a fact. . . . The second and the more important significance of the Incarnation is as an answer to the problem, not of [the] finiteness of man but of his sin, not his involvement in the flux of nature but his abortive efforts to escape that flux."

Part II of *For the Time Being*, "The Annunciation,"
begins inside individual man. The Four Faculties, the
watchers "Over the life of Man" who "manage / His
fallen estate," speak in answer to the Chorus's questions
about the garden. The Four "were once but one," but
with man's Fall they separated and now go their inde-
pendent, contradictory ways. The separation of the
Four represents a split of flesh and spirit, consciousness
and unconsciousness, similar to that which Auden attempted to show in the beginning of the Caliban-Ariel
relationship in *The Sea and the Mirror*. Intuition, "a
dwarf," and Sensation, "a giant," are the animal or unconscious part of man (the sea in *The Sea and the Mirror*), while Feeling, "a nymph," and Thought, "a fairy,"
are the overcontrolled spirit or consciousness (the
desert) of man's life. Together they represent the "Am-
biguous causes / Of all temptation," they "lure man
either / To death or salvation." Like Caliban and Ariel,
they cannot force man to choose hell or heaven. They
merely "look over / The wall of that hidden / Garden,"
and "truthfully tell him / What happens inside." It is up
to man to choose.

Each of the Faculties may look separately into the
garden, but man himself remains outside. The images
which the Faculties use to describe their visions are
understandably extreme, for what they are describing
are visions of hell. Thus when they see Mary walking in
the garden, they relay their messages in a cynical tone.

Through the cynicism of the Faculties, Auden is trying to show that the fractured portions of man's being,
those things he calls his faculties, may glimpse the garden, but these glimpses will be distorted. The Faculties
do not—in fact cannot—envision the breaking of the
silence, because they are *aware* of the silence to begin
with. The Faculties perceive the world distorted from
their own particular angles, and are thus unable to perceive the innocence of Mary. They represent man's desire for knowledge and the results of that desire: frag-
mentation and separation.

With the "Awake" of the Angel Gabriel, the Four Faculties are dismissed. In the eyes of God, Mary is innocent, playing "in a dream of love . . . as all children play." As was pointed out in the "Recitative," there are two types of dream: one, of course, is "your own," the selfish dream of illusion; the second Gabriel identifies as the "dream of love." The childish "dream of love" is a dream of permanence and happiness, "The wish that later they will know / Is tragic and impossible." Yet the dream is true, or was true until the Fall when Eve "turned the flesh Love knew so well / To knowledge of her love. . . ." Since the Fall there are two types of love: Love itself, God, Agape, and love of self, Eros, the adoration of the individual will.[14] Gabriel's message to Mary is that she has the opportunity to bring Love itself and love of self together, to make the dream of childhood's garden "No longer a pretend but true." Mary, by "choosing to / Conceive the Child who chooses you," can restore the relationship. She can give man the chance to stop chasing "The shadow of his images" and to confront "Love's will on earth."

The "Wholly Other" has made his move. Reaching a hand across the abyss, "Today the Unknown seeks the known." Mary must turn the negation of Eve into an affirmation by choosing to accept the opportunity Gabriel presents, for, as she is told, "Love's will requires your own."

This is an extremely important moment in Auden's poetry. It is the moment Caliban was waiting for, the moment that transforms history, that offers man the chance not to understand but to accept life. Understanding what this moment of divine movement means to Auden helps to clarify all of the poetry which follows. The unknown seeking the known does nothing to

[14] Auden says in "Eros and Agape" (a review of *Love in the Western World* by Denis de Rougemont), *The Nation*, June 28, 1941, p. 757: "For Eros surely is . . . the basic will to self-actualization without which no creature can exist, and Agape is that Eros mutated by Grace, a conversion, not an addition, the Law fulfilled, not the Law destroyed."

help man understand his life, and merely knowing about the fact of the seeking does not aid man in living. Malin in *Age of Anxiety*, for instance, knows all about Christ, but the knowledge does not change his life. He feels he understands the meaning of both the Incarnation and the Crucifixion, yet his life is nothing more than meaningless repetition. The understanding of Malin is, in Auden's eyes, no more than the illusion of knowledge because the one essential reality, the manifestation of God in human form, is beyond man's powers of comprehension. Thus the persona of "Horae Canonicae" is saved precisely when he accepts and praises God, man, and existence because he cannot understand. The saint is the man who knows only that he does not know.

So, out of the "darkness and snow" comes Grace, and the world seems to know, as Auden says in a much later poem ("Whitsunday in Kichstetten"), ". . . nothing, except what everyone knows— / if there when Grace dances, I should dance." The "Solo" and "Chorus" which conclude "The Annunciation" sing, dance, and rejoice because finally, at what seemed to be the point of complete negation, it appears as though "There's a Way. There's a Voice."

"The Temptation of Saint Joseph" which follows presents a Joseph who is an ordinary modern man with shoes shined, pants cleaned and pressed, and an "own true Love." When he discovers that Mary is pregnant, and she tells him that the child is God's child, his reaction is one of bewilderment. Moreover, he encounters condescension at every turn. In a bar, the bartender says, "This is on the house." When he asked for the time, "Everyone was very kind." An ass that he sees brays at him, and when he asked the way of a hermit, "He pretended to be asleep." While Joseph relates these occurrences, an offstage Chorus preys on his doubts:

> *Mary may be pure,*
> *But Joseph, are you sure?*

How is one to tell?
Suppose, for instance . . . Well . . .

Finally, caught up with what the world believes and
what he himself also fears, Joseph sits alone in "an
empty house." He feels mocked by the objects that sur-
round him and asks, "Father, what have I done?" He
asks God to answer "The pompous furniture," or at
least to give him one sign of evidence ("one / Important and elegant proof") that God is just and that His
"will is Love."

Gabriel answers him quite simply: "No, you must believe; / Be silent, and sit still." Gabriel thus instructs.
The Narrator then explains to the reader, although he
does not justify. Joseph and Mary, although they are in
what one would consider exceptional circumstances,
must accept the condemnation of the usual, must "be
man and wife / Just as if nothing had occurred" in
order to show that "The Exceptional is always usual /
And the Usual exceptional."

What Auden has effected here is perhaps the neatest
welding together of past and present in the whole of
For the Time Being. Joseph is seen as modern, anxious
man. Afraid of being a cuckold because of both personal pride and fear of public ridicule, he is not given
answers to assuage his fears. Instead, he is told, as
though instructed by Kierkegaard, that he must feel
anxious because man is sinful, and, moreover, he must
praise God not in spite of but because of his anxiety.[15]
Instead of being told, "It is alright, do not worry," he is
asked "To choose what is difficult . . . / As if it were
easy," because "that is faith." Do not ask. "Joseph,
praise."

Joseph is thus the first Christian, the first man who is

[15] See Auden, "Augustus to Augustine," p. 374: "Man chooses
either life or death, but he chooses; everything he does, from going
to the toilet to mathematical speculation is an act of religious
worship, either of God or of himself."

told not to question but to accept the Incarnation, because there is no way for him to understand it. It is no accident that his voice sounds strangely similar to that of the persona of "Horae Canonicae," for Joseph's personality is the one which Auden chooses and develops as his later voice. His "common ungifted nature" becomes Auden's mask.

In the semichoruses and chorus which follow the Narrator, Joseph and Mary are asked to pray for the rest of mankind: for the romantics, the bourgeoisie, the innocent young. They are asked to "Redeem for the dull the / Average way." These choruses show what is most beautiful in the Incarnation to Auden. Both Joseph and Mary were very ordinary human beings. But Mary, because she was chosen, has become "Blessed Woman," and Joseph, because he has accepted without understanding, "Excellent Man." It is through their very ordinariness that Joseph and Mary show the unity of the exceptional and the usual in life. They repair the damage done by the Fall of Adam and Eve. They give man hope through the plainness of their example.

Having presented the supposedly ordinary (Joseph and Mary) and shown why they are not, Auden proceeds in the next section—"The Summons"—to present the supposedly extraordinary, the Three Wise Men. "The Summons" begins with the Star of the Nativity explaining its function. It is "that star most dreaded by the wise, / For they are drawn against their will" to a place "where are no / Footholds for logic. . . ." The Star's purpose is to lead man away from the feeling that he must have answers and to lead him to the realization that there is no answer he can comprehend. The Star, then, is out to destroy man's illusory hope for knowledge, but despite the star's warning the Three Wise Men cannot help but follow it.

After the Wise Men speak, the Star returns to tell them what they must do. The task is far from simple; in fact, it means facing the "lion's mouth" that the Stage

Manager speaks of in *The Sea and the Mirror.* The Wise Men must, as must all Christians, face the fact of death and yet maintain faith. They must, "as the huge deformed head rears to kill, / Answer its craving with a clear I Will." Then, says the Star, they will wake as children "in the rose-garden."

This is, again, an exhortation to believe, but, for the first time in *For the Time Being* it is also a guarantee of what will happen if one believes. Previously we have been given edicts demanding faith, but the Star is offering paradise as a reward for faith.[16]

From the garden of paradise, the Narrator moves us to an introduction of the Just Society; from praising God we move to praising Caesar. Thus, at the actual historical point in time of the Incarnation there is a choice between two summonses, just as in the case of the individual Christian there is always the choice between the secular City of Man and the City of God.

Just as Gabriel and the Star demand a unity of flesh and spirit in individual man, so Caesar demands from society "a concourse of body and concord of soul" to hear "His proclamation." The proclamation demands the registration of all men and their dependents, and states that: "WILFUL FAILURE TO COMPLY WITH THIS ORDER IS PUNISHABLE BY CONFISCATION OF GOODS AND LOSS OF CIVIL RIGHTS."

The contrast between the summons of the Star and that of Caesar is quite clear. Ignoring the summons of the Star means loss of paradise; ignoring the summons of Caesar means loss of this world.[17] The "Fugal

[16] Auden describes the contrast involved in man's choice ("Augustus to Augustine," p. 374): "The contrast is not between body and mind but between flesh, i.e., all man's physical and mental faculties, as they exist in his enslaved self-loving state, and spirit, which witnesses within him to all that his existence was and still is meant to be, capable of loving God in the same way that God loves him."

[17] In the Introduction to *Poets of the English Language,* ed. W. H. Auden and Norman Holmes Pearson (New York: The Viking Press, 1950), III, xxiv–xxv, Auden describes the effect that the

Chorus" which follows Caesar's proclamation gives the reason for choosing Caesar: "He has conquered Seven Kingdoms." He has brought the world of man under one man's control. The needs of this world Caesar can fulfill; therefore, "God must be with Him."

It is not only the world before Christ that Caesar controls, it is also our world. The days when "Mankind is on the march" and which are "stirring times for the editors of newspapers" are our own as well. It is a world of anachronism, of mixed metaphor. The past is the present, and the present is the future, and we might be happy "If we were never alone or always too busy." But the "Perfect State" (the world of Caesar) offers no solace.

As the Narrator puts it, we must "be contrite but without anxiety, / For Powers and Times are not gods but mortal gifts from God." We must choose the Kingdom of Heaven not because it *is*, but because it "may come, not in our present / And not in our future, but in the Fullness of Time." And because it may come, Auden says, "Let us pray" to God, instead of praising Caesar.

The "Chorale" which concludes "The Summons" is the prayer the Narrator asks for. It is a prayer based on man's anxiety, upon the hope "That from our incoherence we / May learn to put our trust in Thee." It is a prayer that man may escape illusion and accept reality without believing that the cures of this world are cures for his basic ailment. The prayer asks for "brutal fact [to] persuade us to / Adventure, Art, and Peace." The key word here is "brutal," for Auden believes that it is only through acceptance of the incredible brutality of

choice of Caesar's world has upon the individual: "In personal life, however, the religion of common sense and good taste is seriously defective. It can neither allow for nor comprehend those decisive once-for-all instants of vision in which a life is confronted by another, addressed by God, Nature, or a Beatrice—which, unique and momentary though they may be, are what make that life a person and give his normal day-to-day experiences their meaning."

this world that man can be led to praise of God. This prayer is Caliban's. He said, "It is just here, among the ruins and the bones, that we may rejoice in the perfected Work which is not ours." The chorale says, "For Thy Goodness even sin / Is valid as a sign." The sound which Caliban asked us to hear, "the real Word," is, in this prayer, "ever legible" evidence that God is ever present.

The Shepherds of the next section, "The Vision of the Shepherds," offer a perfect balance to the Three Wise Men. The Shepherds seem to be natural men, tied to the earth. They are not concerned with the meaning of life, but rather with the "mechanism to keep going" in life. They do not question in the manner of Joseph or the Three Wise Men. Instead of asking, "Why exist?," some "unknown" prompts them into saying, "No, I don't know why, / But I'm glad I'm here." They represent the nondoubting aspect of man's nature, that part of him that asks God only who He is, not why He acts as He does. Unlike the Wise Men, the Shepherds are not concerned with learning; they know only that "What is real / About us all is that each of us is waiting."

The Wise Men were disillusioned in their individual searches for a knowledge that would explain human life. The Shepherds have never searched for knowledge but have merely "minded the store." Yet both feel a lack. The Shepherds and the Wise Men taken together seem to represent external versions of the conscious/ unconscious opposition represented by the Four Faculties. Both Shepherds and Wise Men are waiting, the first group passive, the other active, for "The ingression of Love"; for the assurance that the abyss to which "The Pilgrim Way" has led men is "The Father Abyss" and that it "Is affectionate." Both groups are ready to "run"—they need only be assured that they will *run to love.*

"The Vision of the Shepherds" concludes the first major portion of *For the Time Being*. Auden has now introduced the main characters associated with the birth, and has set the scene physically and symbolically. Beginning with the next section, "At the Manger," we are shown the reactions to the birth.

This section is the climax of *For the Time Being*. Christ is born. The abyss has been crossed and God has become man. All of history and all of space have come together in the "here and now" where "our endless journey stops." We are asked to focus all our attention upon this one moment in time and to see that "Tonight for the first time the prison gates / Have opened."

The journey that the Wise Men and the Shepherds have concluded was one of loneliness; they were all but overcome "With doubts, reproaches, boredom." The journey they are beginning is one of union in which each must bring "this child his body and his mind." To them the Incarnation presents an opportunity to find wholeness and security through adoration. It offers them a chance to love themselves through loving Love [18] and, by exchanging burdens, to love each other. So, Kierkegaard is transformed into Charles Williams.

This emphasis upon love in "At the Manger" is followed by a philosophical explanation of faith in "The Meditation of Simeon." The Wise Men, the Shepherds, and Mary love the child simply because He is there. Simeon gives the intellectual reasons for loving Him. A righteous and devout man, Simeon had been promised by the Holy Spirit that he would not die until he had seen the Savior. He is the questor with his quest completed—he is in the garden, waiting. Thus when he speaks, he speaks as one free from anxiety. His future is assured. He has experienced all of man's doubts, and the present moment is the end of his life.

His "Meditation" is a summary of man's internal life.

[18] As Auden says in "Augustus to Augustine," p. 374: "Man . . . always acts either self-loving just for the hell of it, or God-loving, just for the heaven of it."

He begins with a list of the conditions necessary in the soul of man for the reception of the Incarnation. Then with the revelation that the fear of the *"I Am"* may "here and now" be translated to the love of the *"Thou Art,"* he moves to a series of predictions for the future.

Simeon, a secure version of Eliot's Tiresias, is able to talk about the past, present, and future. For him, "the Time Being" holds no fear at all, because he is certain of its outcome. He is an intellectual who has worked life out, and he presents his conclusions in a logical order. He sees the history of man as consisting of three steps: (1) the state of lingering innocence (the belief that "The Fall had not occurred in fact"); (2) the belief in the life of this world (that Eden was "a childish state which he [man] had permanently outgrown, that the Fall had occurred by necessity"); and (3) the attempts to restore order between the human and Divine (man's hope "that the Fall had occurred by accident"). This survey of history leads Simeon to his list of preconditions for the Incarnation. "Before the Infinite could manifest Itself in the finite," it was necessary that man reach the point of "the ultimate frontier or consciousness" where his knowledge forks off in confusion "towards the One and the Many" and where "nothing should be left that negation could remove."

This is the same point to which Caliban took us "down stage with red faces" in *The Sea and the Mirror.* In fact, Simeon's "Meditation" with its accompanying chorus has the same function in *For the Time Being* that Caliban's speech has in *The Sea and the Mirror:* to make us aware of the current situation. Like the Wise Men and the Shepherds, Simeon is concerned with the "here and now," and his speech is probably the most "unmasked" of all the segments of *For the Time Being.* It is because of the current moment that the past is forgiven and the future redeemed, if, in the current moment, "we pray that, following Him, we may depart from our anxiety into His peace."

When Simeon speaks, he seems to be speaking for the "new" Auden, for his ability to believe that "the Truth is indeed One," that "we are blessed by that Wholly Other Life" of which Caliban spoke. In *The Sea and the Mirror*, Auden follows Caliban's sermon with Ariel's plaintive cry. In *For the Time Being*, he follows Simeon's "Meditation" with Herod's "Meditation." If Simeon speaks for the "new" Auden, Herod is Auden's picture of his "old" self.

Herod is a liberal humanitarian. He believes in man rather than in God—like Dostoevsky's Grand Inquisitor he fears God's presence in human form, for, as he says,

> And suppose . . . that this child is in some inexplicable manner both God and Man, that he grows up, lives, and dies, without committing a single sin? Would that make life any better? On the contrary it would make it far, far worse. For it could only mean this: that once having shown them how, God would expect every man, whatever his fortune, to lead a sinless life in the flesh and on earth.

Herod is Simeon's opposite. Both men are intelligent and logical, but while "logic" leads Simeon to view the history of mankind since the Fall as a step by step progression towards the point of total negation where the Infinite can become manifest in human form, it draws Herod to the conclusion that "the notion of a finite God is absurd." Of course it is absurd. That is precisely Auden's (and Kierkegaard's) point: man must follow logic until it can take him no further, until it leads him to the abyss. Then he must resort to the illogical, to the pure belief that it is nonetheless possible for the abyss to be crossed by the leap into faith. But Herod is unable to do this. He feels that nothing is really wrong with this world and, as a consequence, is in anguish. For this he blames God and brings greater anxiety upon himself, saying finally, "I wish I had never been born."

73

His is the confusion, as Auden sees it, of the introvert; turned in upon himself, he sees the world as he wants to see it, not as it is. To Herod, the "Truth" is not "One" —it is "Many," the many things of this world—and order is the orderly progress of mankind through countless lifetimes.

For "the Time Being," the power of Herod triumphs over the impotence of Simeon, the logic of this world triumphs over that of "that Wholly Other." Defenseless before the power of Herod, Mary and Joseph are driven into flight across the desert into Egypt. The voices of the desert, speaking in rocking, four-beat lines, force them to run the gauntlet of the terrors of this world (*"Where even the dolls go whoring"*) in order to find safety in Egypt, where they will miss their "lost insecurity," the simple humanness they possessed before the birth of Christ. This is the end of the historical pageant of *For the Time Being*. As the Narrator says, again echoing Caliban, "so that is that."

For Auden, this is the human condition. We must "Seek Him in the Kingdom of Anxiety." We must live with the knowledge that, although "We can repress the joy [of the knowledge of the Incarnation], . . . the guilt remains conscious." This is why "The Time Being is . . . the most trying time of all." For having seen God, we must go on *not* seeing Him. We must continue to live our earthly lives outside of paradise, silently, knowing in our silence that "God will cheat no one, not even the world of its triumph."

Yet perhaps we have been given more than we feel we have. In place of the negation of the "Advent" where "The Pilgrim Way" led to the abyss, we are left with the affirmation of the final chorus:

He is the Way
Follow Him through the Land of Unlikeness;
You will see rare beasts, and have unique adventures.

74

He is the Truth
Seek Him in the Kingdom of Anxiety;
You will come to a great city that has expected your
    return for years.

He is the Life.
Love Him in the World of the Flesh;
And at your marriage all its occasions shall dance
    for joy.

Here we have the Way, the Truth, and the Life, and
they may be followed, sought, or lived in *this* world.
Because Christ was made man, because he fulfilled
Mary's fears and took "the Sorrowful Way," man has
been given a chance to see in this world the possibility
of the Other. If Auden intended the beginning of *For
the Time Being* to sound like an ending, the reverse is
certainly true in this concluding chorus. What he offers
here is a possibility, if man can accept it, for the redemption of "the Time Being," not only from insignificance but from negation.

In *The Sea and the Mirror,* Auden played with the
characters of *The Tempest,* using our preconceptions of
their natures to contrast with his own ideas as to what
they would be like without Shakespeare to guide them.
In *For the Time Being,* he uses the situation of the Nativity as a framework within which to present his ideas
as to the meaning of the Incarnation in our own day.
For the Time Being is a much less dramatic work than
The Sea and the Mirror because Auden makes no attempt to make the work visual. If one studies *The Sea
and the Mirror* closely, one is able to visualize the work
staged, to see the characters as characters. On the other
hand, *For the Time Being* is a purely aural work.
There is no need to conjure up scenes in it; in fact, trying to "see" it would only get in the way of compre-

hending the meaning Auden wishes to convey through the delicate balance that he establishes between time past and time present. In *For the Time Being* we are told things; in *The Sea and the Mirror* we are searching for them. The characters in *The Sea and the Mirror* speak in different voices because they are different people. The characters in *For the Time Being* sound different from each other because they represent different qualities. We do not really act in *For the Time Being* because no one really acts.

Auden's search for a "voice" continues. We hear it in the conflict of Simeon and Herod, in the relationship between the Wise Men and the Shepherds, and in the halting, self-conscious lines of Joseph. It is perhaps most evident in Auden's treatment of the Narrator and Chorus. The Narrator is the teacher; like Caliban in the early sections of his speech, he knows and tells but is not involved—he speaks more as a commentator than a participant. The Chorus, however, is very much involved. It carries the theme of *For the Time Being* from the despair of the opening "darkness and snow" to its closing "dance for joy." The Chorus does not comment—it experiences. The Narrator comments but does not experience. Auden's job from here is to unite these two voices. But before he can concentrate on bringing together his new voices, on having a narrator who is also a participant, Auden has one last bit of cleaning up to do: the final elimination of the old persona of the thirties. This he accomplishes through the grotesque execution that is *The Age of Anxiety*.

IV

The Age of Anxiety

The Age of Anxiety, the third of Auden's long, dramatic poems of the 1940s, was published in 1947. Like *The Sea and the Mirror* and *For the Time Being, The Age of Anxiety* deals with man's problems in time and the constant tension he experiences between what is illusory and what is real. But, whereas in *The Sea and the Mirror* and *For the Time Being* Auden took characters and events from outside the present day and dealt with them in relation to the present, in *The Age of Anxiety* Auden uses characters and scenes from the present and through an ornate, highly artificial style tries to give a feeling of universality. In *The Sea and the Mirror* Auden used *The Tempest* as a starting point, counting on our previous associations with the characters to serve as a common ground upon which to build new ideas. In *For the Time Being* he used the scene and situation of the Nativity in much the same manner. In *The Age of Anxiety* the scene is a Third Avenue bar (through much of the work); the time is the Second World War; and the characters are four disaffected moderns.

In the earlier works Auden's problem was much like what Coleridge's was supposed to have been in his contribution to *Lyrical Ballads:* making the reader see "similitude in dissimilitude." Auden set about to make us recognize variants of ourselves, friends, or neighbors in the already familiar characters of *The Tempest* or the Nativity. In *The Age of Anxiety,* however, Auden's

77

task is the reverse—more like Wordsworth's attempt to show "dissimilitude in similitude." Quant, Malin, Emble, and Rosetta are familiar to us in their persons and functions in an immediate, contemporary sense. It is easy for us to believe in Prospero as a magician and in Simeon as a Wise Man because we have known them only in those particular, fictive roles, and all that Auden has to do is to change the fictive relationships slightly so that we associate with them in a different way. With the characters of *The Age of Anxiety*, we must be convinced that these real people are characters; Auden must create a sense of fiction, make us *not* believe in the reality of the situation so that we will attend to a greater reality behind the situation.

Most of the critical complaints about *The Age of Anxiety* lie in finding fault with Auden's methods, his attempts at placing the reader at the necessary fictive distance.[1] The techniques he employs are not really complicated. He calls *The Age of Anxiety* a "Baroque Eclogue." Immediately the word "eclogue" causes an ironic reaction in the reader, for he is asked to superimpose a pastoral setting on four drunks seated in a rundown bar. The irony is increased by Auden's use of the heavy, four-stress Old English meter, which, with its constant alliteration, technically constricts the poem. The reader is pushed back from the reality of the characters and the situation both by the ironic effect of the pastoral and by the artificiality of the verse form. As a result, the poem appears to be a highly contrived work, in a much different sense from any of Auden's other long poems. Instead of being bothered by the intrusion of a slang cliché into an unusual setting (such as

[1] This fault-finding with *The Age of Anxiety* culminates in such final judgments as Randall Jarrell's "*The Age of Anxiety* is the worst thing Auden has written since *The Dance of Death*" ("Verse Chronicle" [a review of *The Age of Anxiety* by W. H. Auden], *The Nation*, October 18, 1947, pp. 424–425), and H. A. Mason's ". . . it is with disappointment that after working through the poem one reflects on the absence of any spark of vitality" ("Mr. Auden's Quartet" [a review of *The Age of Anxiety* by W. H. Auden], *Scrutiny*, XV, 2 [Spring, 1948], 155–160).

Herod's "I brush my teeth every night. I haven't had sex for a month. I object. I'm a liberal"),[2] we are bothered by the extreme formality of construction and language. If Herod, for instance, does not talk enough like Herod but too much like us, Quant, Malin, and the others do not talk enough like us. They are not believable in their situation because they overwhelm it with language. Take for example the beginning of Quant's first speech, an overheard thought as he regards himself in the barroom mirror:

> My deuce, my double, my dear image,
> Is it lively there, that land of glass
> Where song is a grimace, sound logic
> A suite of gestures? [3]

We are asked to believe that this elaborate conceit could come from a widowed shipping clerk. Naturally, it does not; it comes from Auden's conception of what man imagines himself to sound like, of what an ordinary man believes himself capable of saying. Auden attributes the ability of his characters to speak this way to their drinking: "As everyone knows, many people reveal in a state of semi-intoxication capacities which are quite beyond them when they are sober: the shy talk easily and brilliantly to total strangers, the stammerers get through complicated sentences without a hitch, the unathletic is translated into a weight-lifter or a sprinter, the prosaic show an intuitive grasp of myth and symbol." [4]

The Age of Anxiety is a quest poem, perhaps Auden's most elaborate one, yet the quest is false.[5] Its charac-

[2] *Collected Poetry*, p. 460.

[3] W. H. Auden, *The Age of Anxiety* (New York: Random House, 1947), p. 7.

[4] *Ibid.*, pp. 56–57.

[5] For an extensive examination of various types of quests, see Auden's "K's Quest," *The Kafka Problem*, ed. Angel Flores (New York: New Directions, 1946).

ters search within themselves in an attempt to gain self-knowledge, yet their search is doomed from the very beginning because it is induced by external stimulants. *The Age of Anxiety* is a poem that "means" only in the negative sense. The characters search, but do not; their vision is, but is not; the language and ideas are theirs, but are not. They are the damned who refuse to recognize their damnation; they are in Hell but believe themselves to be only in Purgatory. A more legitimate complaint about *The Age of Anxiety* than those about its tone would seem to be that Auden tries to give a picture of the modern human condition which denies possibility but refuses to call it impossible.

In a cursory examination, *The Age of Anxiety* appears to be a dramatic amplification of Auden's earlier poem, "September 1, 1939." The earlier work, as we have seen, depicts the shock and dislocation suffered at the beginning of a war, as shown through the reflections of one man sitting in a bar on 52nd Street. The unbelievable has happened, and man is cast adrift from that in which he has held faith. His faith, in fact, is dead, and belief in the good has been replaced by the existence of evil. Man has become afraid that his feeling of his own goodness is, like the goodness of mankind, a mere fiction. He turns, desperately, searching for "Ironic points of light" and prays that he may "Show an affirming flame." [6]

By the time of *The Age of Anxiety*, even that faint hope is gone. The war which began with "September 1, 1939" is in full swing, and the "lights" are gathered together as the characters of *The Age of Anxiety*. In "September 1, 1939," the bar appears to be a temporary stop, a place to rest and gain the strength necessary for the battle, much like Prospero's island. In *The Age of Anxiety* the bar is all there is. The time is one of real war, and the bar has become an end in itself, instead of merely a false stopping place. It offers the possibility of

[6] Auden, *Collected Poetry*, p. 59.

escape into illusion, it gives its customers the possibility of believing that things are not what they are, that life is not life. *The Sea and the Mirror* began with its characters about to leave the illusion of their island, about to enter into life. There is hope in that work, because, in spite of the odds, there is hope in the characters. Naïve, sophisticated, or humble, they are earnest about their lives. In *The Age of Anxiety* any attempt to leave the island is hallucinatory, induced by liquor. The voyages of the characters are taking them further from life rather than drawing them deeper into it. They cannot be earnest, and as a consequence their quest is mock, an attempt which can end only in foolishness and failure. Quant, Malin, Rosetta, and Emble do not want reality; they want escape, yet this is impossible.

Quant, as has been mentioned earlier, begins the action of *The Age of Anxiety* by addressing his image in the mirror. This is typically (as well as stereotypically) a drinker's action. Facing the self that is not the self, the double, the "dear image" of the mirror, is much easier than forcing one's attention on the real self. It is possible to hold back the real problem by simply commenting on appearance. The mirror can always lie by offering man the chance not to believe that what he sees is himself; it enables him to believe that the real self might be "the poet disguised." [7] Quant is an aging, homosexual widower whose lack of legitimate experience has rendered him impotent in relation to life. His

[7] Auden says elsewhere in regard to the relationship of the mirror to art: "Art, as the late Professor R. G. Collingwood pointed out, is not Magic, i.e., a means by which the artist communicates or arouses his feelings in others, but a mirror in which they may become conscious of what their own feelings really are: its proper effect, in fact, is disenchanting.

"By significant detail it shows us that our present state is neither as virtuous nor as secure as we thought, and by the lucid pattern into which it unifies these details, its assertion that order is *possible*, it faces us with the command to make it actual." W. H. Auden, "The Poet of the Encirclement" (a review of *A Choice of Kipling's Verse*, ed. T. S. Eliot), *The New Republic*, October 25, 1943, pp. 579–581.

only responses are simpering self-admonitions ("Why, Miss ME, what's the matter?") or limp excuses. The mirror interests him because it offers him the easiest way of facing himself.

Malin, the second character to appear, is the dominant character of the work. He is on leave from the Canadian Air Force where he is a medical intelligence officer, and in the world of *The Age of Anxiety* he is both the would-be doctor and the leader. His name is important, for he is—in terms of the war outside—a malingerer, and there is more than a hint of the satanic in his make-up.

Rosetta, a department store buyer, is the most human of the characters, and in her long soliloquy at the conclusion of Part V she comes very close to a moment of genuine self-realization. The fourth character, Emble, is a young sailor. He is the would-be prince, and much of the action in *The Age of Anxiety* leads up to his prospective sexual union with Rosetta. His failure in this—he achieves only the oblivion of sleep—is the act which (ironically) climaxes the work.

Part I, entitled "Prologue," introduces the scene and the characters. Each character begins by thinking "out loud" in soliloquies meant to reveal character. Quant, for instance, looks at himself with false admiration and is even a bit awed at his imaginary idea of his own mystery. Malin, coolly intelligent, examines the theoretical nature of man. Rosetta, unhappy with herself and her present, endeavors to create an imaginary and happy past. And Emble, feeling himself isolated from his fellows, passes his youthful judgment on their follies. The characters seem to balance one another: Quant's imaginary present with Rosetta's imaginary past—both illusions, both intensely personal—and Malin's comments on man in general with Emble's remarks on the particular people in the bar—both objective, both at least attempting to deal with the immediate world. Yet these relationships merely seem to be, and the four characters are definitely alone in this opening scene, isolated within their separate thoughts.

It is the radio which brings them together. Auden has used the radio with ironic effect before (see, in particular, *The Ascent of F6*), but its use here is not merely ironic; it is destructive or, even perhaps, corrective. The call of the radio is not the call of God nor that of man. Rather, it is an impersonal, dehumanized call. The voice delivers an "official doctored message," listing the horrors of the slaughter of the day just passed. Its intrusion forces the characters to adapt their thoughts to a common theme: "Many have perished; more will." They are united by a confrontation with death. Thus, when the radio concludes its grisly enumeration with a wartime commercial ("Buy a bond. Blood saves lives. / Donate now. Name this station"), they are driven to speak to each other. They talk about the horrors of the present in which, Rosetta says, "Numbers and nightmares have news value," and Malin then adds, "A crime has occurred, accusing all."

In response to these condemnations Emble presents the liberal attitude (which is Auden's old position and which, interestingly, is taken here by the youngest, most naïve character, damning it almost as much as it was damned in *For the Time Being* when Herod held forth in much the same vein), saying "Better this than barbarian misrule." He cites history to illustrate the innocence of the civilized, who dwell "at ease / In their sown centers, sunny their minds, / Fine their features," and the guilt of the uncivilized, the "Peripheral people, rancid ones / Stocky on horses." Malin replies that in the present age there is no innocence, that the city is as guilty as the wasteland. There is no escape from the fact of war within reality; we are all responsible because we are alive.

Their conversation on man's damnation is interrupted by the radio which sounds again, this time sending forth an angel chorus of commercials which bring "tidings of great joy." Malin reacts to the radio with intellectual fury and demands a quest, for although their bodies are "bound to these bar-room lights, / The night's odors, the noise of the El . . . ," their "thoughts are free." All that needs to be found is a direction in which they may wander. Malin poses the possibilities of the past and future, both of which are rejected, and finally offers the present. What he in fact proposes is that they offer—by and for themselves—a play on man's nature, a drama based on their own individual experiences as that "fallen soul / With power to place, to explain every / What in his world but why he is neither / God nor good."

The radio interrupts once again, demanding to know "HOW ALERT ARE YOU," but is silenced by Quant who announces the presentation of:

HOMO ABYSSUS OCCIDENTALIS

or

A CURIOUS CASE OF COLD FEET

or

SEVEN SELFISH SUPPERLESS AGES

The characters move from their bar stools to a booth, and the play which constitutes the body of *The Age of Anxiety* is ready to begin.

Part II of *The Age of Anxiety*, "The Seven Ages," serves as the first act. Malin dominates this section, acting as a guide and, through his introductions to each of the ages, controlling the characters' reactions. He describes each age and sets the tone for response. The others give substance to his theories, drawing on experiences from their own pasts, presents, and hypothetical futures. The effect of this technique is to cast Malin as the Tempter. He speaks not of himself but of universals, forcing his companions not only to reveal themselves but to see their own lives merely as examples which prove his theories. He is the false or, at best, one-sided hero. He knows something that is, or seems to be, true about life, but his knowledge is not connected to his life. He is able to describe, yet he does not, like Caliban, stand "down stage" with his companions. He is a disconnected priest, separated from his flock.

At the beginning of "The Seven Ages," he asks us to "Behold the infant"; we feel him to be looking at us as if *we* were that infant, while his own infancy remains inviolable or seems even nonexistent. What he says is, for Auden, true; it is the *manner* in which he says it that puzzles. He describes the state of infancy in almost Wordsworthian terms. The child is "helpless in cradle and / Righteous still"; yet, and Auden here is closer in thought to Freud than to Wordsworth, he already has a "Dread in his dreams." The child knows nothing of the leap before him, yet "He jumps and is judged: he joins mankind, / The fallen families, freedom lost, / Love becomes Law." [8] From innocence to experience is such a simple step—merely the process of becoming conscious, and then self-conscious. The innocent becomes the guilty, "A foiled one learning / Shyness and shame, a shadowed flier." This familiar Audenesque picture of the flier concludes Malin's description of the state of being in the first age, the "Fall" of each man, and sets the scene for the responses of the other characters.

Quant, the first to speak, remembers his modern childhood. His recollections seem almost an intentional mockery of Dylan Thomas; the "hammerpond" where the children swam was "green and grim" with "dank water" in which, although without joy, they "Swam without swearing." The world of nature became for them the world of the smelting mill, an ugly world, "black with burnt grass," a world where man has conquered nature and destroyed it, leaving nothing for his

[8] For another version of this Eros-Logos relationship, see Auden's poem "Law like Love" in *Collected Poetry*, pp. 74–76.

children.[9] It is the reality of the dream of "New styles of architecture."

Malin's suggestions turn Rosetta to her dream of what her past should have been. Bitterly ashamed of the tawdry mediocrity of her real childhood in a "semi-detached / Brick villa in Laburnum Crescent," she has constructed the childhood she always wanted, complete with picnics and a father "Tall in tweeds on the terrace gravel."

These recollections of childhood, whether real or imagined, bring into ugly reality the theme introduced by Malin. Life, for these children was "grim," "dank," "hot," "heavy," "black," "cruel," "vacant," "untidy"; their world was peopled with cruel cousins, who were "Strong and stupid," or with "helpless babies." Rosetta's escape into fantasy seems justified; so does Emble's hole in the "back garden." Anything seems preferable to Quant's celebration of the "secret meetings at the slaughter-house."

The second age of man, as Malin describes it, is youth. No longer a child let loose among unfriendly giants, the youth moves out into life. This is the age when man first realizes that "He has laid his life-bet with a lying self." Yet his naïve belief in himself and in his place in life is boundless. He knows that he is special and that the great hold a "promised chair / In their small circle" for him. He must only reach it. He is in love with himself not as he is, but as he knows he will be—with his becoming, not his being. If childhood is as

[9] A bitter explanation of this world is presented in Auden's poem "1929" (*Collected Poetry*, pp. 62–68), where he says in part:

> A 'bus ran home then, on the public ground
> Lay fallen bicycles like huddled corpses:
> No chattering values of laughter emphasized
> Nor the swept gown ends of a gesture stirred
> The sessile hush; until a sudden shower
> Fell willing into grass and closed the day.
> Making choice seem a necessary error.

the characters indicate it to be, the age of discontent with the present, youth is the age of belief in the possibility of the future. The memories of Quant, Rosetta, and Emble seem to bear this out. Quant, for instance, tells of his private vision of himself when as "a bus-boy brushing a table / Sullen and slight," he saw himself to be "A cleaned tycoon in a cooled office." Rosetta tells of seeing in her youthful dreams her "house on the headland," and of "putting forth / Alone in my launch through a low tunnel / Out to the ocean." And Emble recalls that after fighting with his father he "supplied the words / For a fine dirge which fifty years hence / Massed choirs would sing as my coffin passed, / Grieved for and great on a gun-carriage." All are dreams, and each is typical of the dreamer: Quant, the clerk-to-be, dreams of being a tycoon; Rosetta, oppressed by her family's mediocrity, dreams of the glamour of magnificent possessions; and Emble, unloved and bullied, dreams of the effect his death will have ("Then they'll realize how much they *really* loved me").

The next age is that of sexual awakening, when man must cut off his dream images as "he learns what real / Images are." He may have dreamed of love, but here he encounters the actual presence of another, and, in the process of "learning to love, at length he is taught / To know he does not." This is a bitter notion, but in the world of *The Age of Anxiety* there is no such thing as love. Sexual attraction becomes ludicrous as, "Blind on the bride-bed, the bridegroom snores." The problem here is that one's Eros is bound to conflict with another's as long as it remains merely Eros. Eros is not human love but self-love. In order for man to find fulfillment, to join in the coinherence, his Eros must be mutated by Grace into Agape. This, of course, is beyond the characters of *The Age of Anxiety;* they are far from being real "points of light." As a result, they are only able to ridicule this age. Quant tells a not-so-pretty little story of his "Visitor's voyage to Venus Island," and the songs of Rosetta and Emble offer no better pictures of young love.

The fourth age takes us back to the circus imagery of *The Sea and the Mirror*. There Auden used the circus as a form of art too close to life to have any purgative effect on the audience. Here he uses it as life itself, ordinary life with the illusions of personal fulfillment taken from it. Our life in this world is, as Rosetta terms it, an "Impermanent appetitive flux," and the world itself no more than a "clown's cosmos."

Emble takes this circus imagery a step further. He sees mankind grouped in families which are "Pent in the packed compulsory ring / Round father's frown." Each man "waits his / Day to dominate," yet, when given the chance, he does nothing different, he only follows the act which precedes. It is much easier to "mimic the Middle Way" than it is to strike off in new directions. It is much easier to content oneself with "a fuzzy hope . . . that sometime all this / Will walk away" than it is to force the issue, to confront "The Absolute Instant."

Malin presents man in the fifth age as "an astonished victor, . . . at last / Recognition surrounds his days." He feels as though he has made his peace with the meaning of life. His anxiety seems to lessen as "He learns to speak / Softer and slower, not to seem so eager." He no longer feels trapped in the circus ring and ruled by a mob; he now finds the world a dull, bland place.

Emble, however, caught up in his own youth, refuses to move so swiftly into stagnant middle age. He demands to know why Malin and the others must "Leave out the worst / Pang of youth." What youth wants most is to know what will happen. Afraid of time, youth asks, "Shall we ever be asked for? Are we simply / Not wanted at all?" Emble is the only one of the characters who is still bound by youth; as Auden describes him earlier, he suffers "from that anxiety about himself and his future which haunts, like a bad smell, the minds of most young men." [10] He is disturbed by time in a different way from Quant or Rosetta, for he is still young enough to demand a future from the world—he wants an answer from Caesar, from the world.

Quant, replying to Emble, wags a finger and tells him that soon he "will no longer / Expect more pattern, more purpose than / Your finite fate." This Rosetta refuses to accept. She still demands purpose and results in man's battle with time, she wants to know where we are going as "we go on talking, / Many about much, but remain alone." Her complaint is really no more than a variation on Emble's. Perhaps time is more frustrating to her since she has travelled through more of it, but Rosetta and Emble face the same problem: caught up in life, they demand a future better than the present, but where is it?

Quant says, "Nowhere." There is no future because we live always in the present where hope can never be realized. Life goes nowhere because there is nowhere for it to go. This, the fifth age, is the most depressing because it is Quant's. He dominates it and tries to eliminate all hope. His attitude is that if man cannot adjust to mediocrity, it is too bad. That is all there is. If man asks for more, the world only gets worse.

So, by the sixth age, man, the anxious, mediocre creature, begins to show his age. The road to mediocrity is almost complete, and now man can only pine "for some / Nameless Eden where . . . the children play . . . / Since they needn't know they're not happy." Impotent, aged, and successful, Malin's man of the sixth age is past the point of worrying and almost past the point of caring.

By the time Malin reaches the seventh age, his hypothetical man is tired out; "His last illusions have lost patience / With the human enterprise." The other char-

[10] *The Age of Anxiety,* p. 6.

acters have passed the point of personal involvement; none of them is ready to die just yet. So they examine the future, both their own and that of general man. Rosetta says that for all men "Poor and penalized [is] the private state." Emble adds a personal note: "Must I end like that?"

With the conclusion of "The Seven Ages," Auden's intent in *The Age of Anxiety* begins to emerge. He wishes to give us a picture of the damned in a world gone mad. Malin, the prospective priest, seems no priest at all, but a malicious psychoanalyst. He knows what is wrong with life but not how to cure it. He is able to bring the other characters out, to get them to confess their failings and hostilities, but he is unable to offer them a better way.

The importance of the fact that Auden has chosen to make Malin a medical intelligence officer, interested in "laboratory and lecture-hall," must not be overlooked. Malin is an "old" Auden hero, and his voice is the "old" Auden voice suddenly gone flat. He is a composite of the qualities Auden once admired, and yet he has essentially nothing to offer in terms of a genuine or positive solution; he can only comment, expose, destroy. He leads the other characters, his patients, blindly along a dead-end path.

After the presentation of man in the seventh age, the characters separate briefly, with Malin repairing to the men's room, Rosetta and Emble losing themselves in their particular thoughts, and Quant going to the bar for drinks where once again he confronts himself in the mirror. Things have happened to Quant since the last confrontation; now, instead of "my dear image," his reflection is a "Dear friend of a friend" who should "Beware my weakness." In short, Quant has become afraid.

The next phase of their journey is through space rather than time. They have seen, through Malin's guided tour, that man's movement through life leads only to death, not to happiness. Perhaps contentment lies in the other direction, in finding the "Regressive road to Grandmother's House." By travelling through life as though it were a landscape, man might find "that state of prehistoric happiness," "The Quiet Kingdom."

The first act of their play ends with the authors/ actors dissatisfied with what they have discovered. Having tried to examine what the past, present, and future mean to each of them, they have seen nothing save the horror of the process of aging until death. The journey through "The Seven Ages" was a realistic one, composed by a group of people sitting and talking about their separate real or imagined experiences. "The Seven Stages," the second act of the play done by the characters of *The Age of Anxiety*, is completely non-realistic. In order to perform it, the characters try to submerge themselves into a group organism. As Auden says: "The more completely these four forgot their surroundings and lost their sense of time, the more sensitively aware of each other they became, until they achieved in their dream that rare community which is otherwise only attained in states of extreme wakefulness. But this did not happen all at once." [11] "The Seven Ages" was an attempt to find the perfect time of life, the age of innocence, fulfillment, or peace at which a man could be content to stop. "The Seven Stages" is an attempt to find home, the place where man can stay. Just as there was no time, there is no place.

"The Seven Stages," in the dramatic context of *The Age of Anxiety*, is a search for the proper stage (in the theatrical sense) from which to present a play. Man, to Auden, is essentially a bad actor constantly dissatisfied with both his role and the sets. Each of the stages in "The Seven Stages" is a possible setting within which the characters could act out their lives' dramas, and yet each is unsatisfactory; at each stop they feel driven into movement.

[11] *Ibid.*, p. 57.

In the first stage of the characters' journey, each of them is alone, isolated with his own thoughts: "At first all is dark and each walks alone." This is the way that every journey—symbolic or real—begins, and, although the characters do not realize it yet, this is the way that each false journey ends. Their journey, then, because it is a false journey, is a journey to nowhere.

At this point, the only thing the characters share is a "feeling of remoteness and desertion." Like the Chorus of *For the Time Being*, they are afraid of both the external world ("Mountains menace my life") and their own internal problems ("I've a horror of dwarfs / And a streaming cold"). They are also frightened of being alone, so, coupling "youth with youth and age with age," they move from "the high heartland to the maritime plains."

This first pairing initiates the second stage of the journey and is important to the journey as a whole because it shows both the possibility and the futility of hope. Malin and Quant, the old, really have no hope; they are past caring or believing. However, Emble and Rosetta, the young, do have hope, for Emble in particular still cares, still believes that a meaningful journey is possible. As a young man, he considers himself to be among the exceptional, who differ from the ordinary, and he clings to his journey as a means of distinguishing himself. It is evident, however, that his is a journey towards what is not, and his desire to make the journey seems to come more from a fear of failure than from a genuine desire for the quest. His is a feeling of youthful insecurity disguised in the glamour of being different. As this second stage of the journey ends, it becomes apparent that there is no escape from self, either through the romance of youth that Emble and Rosetta typify, or through the resignation to age that we see in Malin and Quant.

As the couples turn inland, Emble and Rosetta by plane, Malin and Quant by train, the third stage of the journey begins, and a different path to escape is explored. Here, once again, is Auden's favorite separation of the exceptional and the ordinary. To Rosetta and Emble their trip by private plane renews the possibility of escape, for they feel that by skill they have escaped the "public prison" of human life. Yet they still feel anxious, for some fear forces them

> To make in miniature
> That earth anew, and now
> By choice instead of chance
> To suffer from the same
> Attraction and untruth,
> Suspicion and respect.

They are forced to realize once again that there is no escape from life, for if man does succeed in escaping those around him, he merely recreates the circumstances of life in his new environment.

In juxtaposition with the flight of Emble and Rosetta is the train journey of Quant and Malin. Just as Emble and Rosetta find they cannot escape life by flying above it, so Quant and Malin find they cannot escape it by ironically immersing themselves in it. In spite of the knowledge that they are surrounded by "melancholics mewed in their dumps," "short blowhards," or all "the successful smilers the city can use," they still despair of the possibility of any kindness in the world and feel that the only available guide is no more than a "mad oracle."

High or low, by attempted escape or attempted immersion, the characters complete the third stage of their journey still failures as they arrive in the city. Malin speaks for them all in commenting on the city. It is an ugly place, the seat of a "facetious culture" with its "Publishing houses, pawnshops and pay toilets." The people are no better than the place in Malin's eyes, and all he really wants to know about them is "How are these people punished?"

From the city they take a trolley car northward to "the big house," which is the end of the journey's fourth stage. Rosetta's fantasy since her unhappy childhood has been of the mansion in which she wishes she had been reared and to which she feels she will return. It is no wonder, then, that it is she who exclaims on sighting "the big house," "In I shall go, out I shall look."

While she is within, the others wait, examining the outside. Quant says, "The facade has a lifeless look." The house is, of course, the human body, with its "book-lined rooms at the back" serving as the brain and "the guards at the front gate [who] / Change with the seasons" serving as the senses. Man, as he contemplates his house from the outside, is a sorry creature; he cannot even conceal his failings, for the outside world watches his "ruined kitchen-maids / Blubber behind the bushes."

Within the house it is no better, as Rosetta reports on her return. In her desire to see life and the world in their proper perspective, inside the big house of her dreams Rosetta has unwittingly forced herself to see life as it is, complete with all its agony and ugliness. Of her vision she says, "I would gladly forget; let us go quickly." In Rosetta's experience, "The significant note is nature's cry / Of long-divided love," for although she does not understand it, Rosetta has seen Auden's version of the world without Christ. It is a world of "malice" and "greed" where "things" are "thrown into being," and the cry of "long-divided love" is the separation of man from God, the existence of Eros without Agape.

After a short race, the characters arrive at the "forgotten graveyard," which is the end of the fifth stage. The graveyard is a "still / Museum [exhibiting] / The results of life." Yet, even here life begins again, for around the dead

> Flittermice, finches
> And flies restore
> Their lost milieu.

94

These "occasional creatures," the opposite of poor, desperate, unoccasional man, "Blindly, playfully" bridge "death's eternal gap" with their simple "quotidian joy." The difference between man and the rest of nature is put quite plainly. Man does not bridge the "gap" playfully, he does not breed in graveyards, or at least he would like to think he does not.

Once again, the characters pair off, this time Rosetta with Quant and Emble with Malin. No one is happy with this arrangement and so, during the sixth stage of the journey, they talk to themselves instead of to each other. Their thoughts, instead of merely being self-concerned, are directed in alternately pitying and desirous ways towards their companions. By this stage, the sixth, they have become aware not only of themselves and their companions, but also of their comparative desires within the group. Emble and Rosetta feel they want each other and feel guilty about it; Malin and Quant recognize the desires of Rosetta and Emble, yet feel the demands of their own desires as well. All that remains for the characters to do is to face this new pairing and its concomitant absurdity.

This they begin to do as they confront the temptations of the hermetic gardens. Emble is willing, perhaps, to try the possibilities, illusions, and realities of the gardens, and, out of desperation, even Rosetta is willing; but Quant and Malin are not: "They become uneasy and unwell." The charm of the gardens, offering the possibility of action, seems to the characters to be an accusation, a ridicule of their impotence. They begin to feel guilty. Emble remembers his "mother's grief" and the fact that he "pencilled on envelopes / Lists of my loves." Quant remembers wishing his wife dead and then turning her over. Rosetta says that she "must pay for thinking / Failure funny," and Malin says, "I have felt too good / At being better than the best of my colleagues." Gathering their guilt and the resultant imaginary physical ills, "they plunge into the labyrinthine forest and vanish down solitary paths, with no guide but their sorrows, no companion but their own voices," as they begin the seventh and final stage of the journey. They wander through the forest, despairing of their ills, begging mercy. Finally they meet at the forest's edge where they are confronted by the desert, which represents the completion of the first half of the seventh stage.

Their journey of escape is almost done. They began with water, a symbolic birth, and they must end with sand, a symbolic death. However, the desert means more to Auden in this context than merely death. In their fear of the wastes of the desert the characters see mirrored all their fears of living: to cross the desert is to make the journey through a lifetime in the world. Confronted by the prospect of entering into the "Rainless regions," as Quant describes the desert, the "ancestral wastes, / Lands beyond love," they begin to have very real doubts and fears. Malin says: "It takes will to cross this waste / Which is really empty." Then he asks the central secular question of *The Age of Anxiety*:

> Do I love this world so well
> That I have to know how it ends?

As they stand, caught by this question and the sudden fear that there really is no meaning, no positive solution to the problem of existing, their journey completes itself before their eyes: the desert turns into the real world "from which their journey has been one long flight," and their quest for escape ends in a hallucinatory exaggeration of the horrors of reality. What they see, as Emble identifies it for them, is "A grinning gap, a growth of nothing / Pervaded by vagueness."

So, their mock quest completed, their worst fears realized, they end their play, wake up, and leave the bar.[12]

12 Auden, in "K's Quest," describes what he calls the "Dream (or Divine Comedy) Quest," and in so doing, describes the positive

In "September 1, 1939," Auden referred to mankind as being "Lost in a haunted wood." Yet in that poem, "Faces along the bar" could find some escape and "Cling to their average day." Here, at the conclusion of "The Seven Stages" section of *The Age of Anxiety*, we see what happens if man lets go of that "average day" and tries to explore the "haunted wood." Auden employs the drunkenness of the characters in a very definite manner. Drink stands as a metaphor for delusion. The characters do not want to face themselves as they are, so they set out on an imaginary journey hoping to find the cure for their malaise. Unfortunately, the journey takes them inside the framework of their relationship with the world and the delusion cracks apart, intensifying and refracting the horrors of life like a bad case of the d.t.'s

The remaining three sections of *The Age of Anxiety* follow the characters from the bar to their homes. They do not have exact memories of their journey through the seven stages, and instead of the despair they felt at the conclusion of the journey, they now have a vague urge for companionship. They all accept Rosetta's invitation, actually extended only to Emble, to go to her apartment for a final drink. While in a cab on the way to her apartment, they compose the lament which constitutes Part IV of *The Age of Anxiety*, "The Dirge."

Having completed their journey through the life and country of man, and having found no hope inherent in either man or nature, they have come to the conclusion that life could not have continued so long "had not some semi-divine stranger with superhuman powers

version of the quest of the seven stages. He says (pp. 48–49): "The purpose of the journey is no object but spiritual knowledge, a vision of the reality behind appearances, while the dreamer, when he wakes, can henceforth live his life on earth. The dreamer is, theoretically, everyman, i.e., it is not by any act or virtue of his that he attains this vision, for the vision is a gift of Divine Grace. It does not necessarily follow that the vision will change his life, but if he does not change, his responsibility is greater than that of those who have never been granted his vision."

. . . appeared from time to time to rescue both [man and nature], for a brief bright instant, from their egregious destructive blunders." It is the absence of such a "savior" in their present day that they lament. The characters have learned nothing from their journeys. Instead of searching within themselves for the answers to the problems that they face, they can only bemoan the lack of a leader, a hero. Their god, hero, or savior is the kindly, "fix-it" parent. Like Stephano of *The Sea and the Mirror,* they want someone to assume the responsibility for their own errors, to "dust / The cobwebbed kingdoms now." What they do not want is a god or leader who will demand an activity on their own part equal to his own. They want a lawgiver, but a "lawgiver [who] lies below his people, / Bigger bones of a better kind." Ideally, the "semi-divine stranger" would bring laws and heal, and then quietly die, or, in other words, be the perfect False Messiah.

Part V of *The Age of Anxiety* is entitled "The Masque." It is in this section that the action of the work is climaxed. In a long introductory paragraph, Auden says of his characters and, by extension, of all mankind:

> Had they been perfectly honest with themselves, they would have had to admit that they were tired and wanted to go home alone to bed. That they were not was in part due, of course, to vanity, the fear of getting too old to want fun or too ugly to get it, but also to unselfishness, the fear of spoiling the fun for others. Besides, only animals who are below civilization and the angels who are beyond it can be sincere. Human beings are, necessarily, actors who cannot become something before they have first pretended to be it; and they can be divided, not into the hypocritical and the sincere, but into the sane who know they are acting and the mad who do not.

98

One of the ideas Auden is particularly concerned with in the long works of the forties is the relationship between actor and character, or man and his mask. He feels that it is most human to pick a guise to wear or to choose a particular role to play in life. The great danger to sanity lies in confusing the chosen role with reality, in believing with Antonio that we are what we pretend we are rather than what we really are. This is the problem that Caliban spoke of in *The Sea and the Mirror*, and it is the problem faced by the characters of *The Age of Anxiety* as they present "The Masque."

In the earlier sections of *The Age of Anxiety*, the characters tried to escape the problems of life through a make-believe quest. To Auden's mind, this is psychologically dangerous for, as he showed at the conclusion of "The Seven Stages," the real world cannot be escaped or altered by such an attempt. Yet even so, the dream of escape is not nearly so dangerous as believing that one can change the real world by merely willing change; after all, the dream can always be forgotten or hidden, but the real world cannot. We see the dangers of trying to bring man's will to bear on reality in the doomed attempt of Rosetta and Emble to realize the "sweet shared secret" of their dreams.

The tone of "The Masque" is intentionally satiric. In spite of their hopes, the characters know that they are acting; they are only momentarily deluded, not mad. They are making one last attempt to believe that Eros is "the answer" and that it is manifested in sexual intercourse.

Rosetta opens "The Masque" by turning on the radio which promises *"savage selections / By brutal bands from bestial tribes"* that *"Will drag you off to their dream retreats / To dance with your deaths till the dykes collapse."* After this bitter introduction, the selections begin, and Rosetta and Emble dance. In the course of their dancing, the attraction between them becomes more obvious "and of immense importance." As both dancers and spectators recognize this, they all begin a masque which is both a mock marriage mass and a fertility rite.

Malin, once again acting the priest, begins by "building a little altar of sandwiches" upon which he places an olive, and then he offers an invocation to Venus. With this mock prayer as a beginning, Emble and Rosetta commence the exchange of vows. Emble addresses her as "My carnal care," and she addresses him as "My doom, my darling." Their vows continue through a long exchange in which Emble gives an extreme exaggeration of the husband as knight-like hero ("If you whisper, I'll wage wars") and Rosetta a caricature of the doting housewife ("When you're on edge, I'll empty your ash-trays"). Following Quant's libation (pouring the dregs of a glass on the carpet), invocation of "the local spirits" (" ye little larvae . . . / Potty, P-P . . ."), and obscene blessing of the couple ("O rest on his rock in your red dress . . . O stiffly stand, a staid monadnock, / On her peneplain"), all the characters join together in a chorus which describes the glory that the union of Emble and Rosetta will bring to the world.

With this hope for a redemption in sexual terms for the agonies of the world, Quant and Malin exit, accompanied by Rosetta. Once she has seen them to the elevator, she returns to her apartment and finds Emble passed out on her bed. She realizes that he is not at fault, that he did try ("You danced so bravely") as long as the illusion of romance was just that and nothing more. The trouble came, she feels, when she tried to make the mock marriage into a real one, when, instead of making believe she was his "dish," she began to wish that she really were.

In her soliloquy, Rosetta casts herself as the Wandering Jew in opposition to Emble's Christian Knight. While she is transient and sits "waiting / On my light

luggage to leave if called / For some new exile . . . ,"
he will "build here, be / Satisfied soon . . . / With
some glowing girl." She only hopes that for his own
sake, "As long as you live may your lying be / Poetic
only." [13] She both envies and loathes him for his naïve
"Christian luck," for his future where "Niceness is all
and / The rest bores." [14] She sees his passing out as an
escape into a world which she will never share nor
understand.

From this point on, the subject of Rosetta's soliloquy
is no longer Emble and herself, but herself alone. She
sees no hope in self-delusion, for no matter how hard
she tries to run, God the Father, like the Hound of
Heaven, will pursue. Her lies have been multiple, her
life imaginary, yet the real has never really been hidden
from the guilt she feels is God. As she says:

> My fears are before Him; He'll find all,
> Ignore nothing. He'll never let me
> Conceal from Him the semi-detached
> Brick villa in Laburnum Crescent,
> The poky parlor, the pink bows on
> The landing-curtains, or the lawn mower
> That wouldn't work.

Unlike her public face, her private face, the one she
calls her god's,

[13] Auden says in "Nature, History and Poetry," p. 418: "In a poem
as distinct from many other verbal societies, meaning and being are
identical. Like an image in the mirror, a poem might be called a
pseudo-person, i.e., it has uniqueness and addresses the reader as
person to person, but, like all natural beings, and unlike historical
persons, it cannot lie."

[14] Compare this to the Stage Manager in *The Sea and the Mirror:*
> All the rest is silence
> On the other side of the wall;
> And the silence ripeness
> And the ripeness all.
> (*Collected Poetry,* p. 352)

. . . won't pretend to
Forget how I began, nor grant belief
In the mythical scenes I make up
Of a home like theirs, the Innocent Place where
His Law can't look.

She knows that there will be no peace for her, no escape from her guilt unless she is able to face herself as
she is and her past as it was; she says: "I shan't be at
peace / Till I really take your restless hands, / My poor
fat father." Yet the peace she asks for is impossible.
There is no forgiveness because there is really nothing
to forgive. Recognition in Rosetta's case is simply regret. She failed because she failed, and there is nothing
to be done about it. This recognition is painful, but it is
not positive because there is nowhere for her to go. Her
soliloquy leaves the reader feeling that in her life to
come she will find that, as she herself puts it, "More
boys like this one may embrace me, yet / I shan't find
shelter."

The "Epilogue" which comprises Part VI and concludes *The Age of Anxiety* is composed of alternating
choruses of "an impromptu ballad" which Quant sings
to himself while walking home, and the thoughts of
Malin as he rides the subway home. Quant's snatches of
song seem to make up a cynical commentary on man's
foibles through history. His song is a war ballad which
makes fun of the inhumanity of the various committees
and subcommittees of "the Victory Powers" as they
foolishly chop up the holdings of the defeated, such
action being brought to the attention of the public by
"Commentators who broadcast by the courtesy of a
shaving cream."

The thoughts of Malin as he proceeds homeward are
as different from Quant's flippancies as Rosetta's attempt at self-examination is from Emble's blocking out
of consciousness. Malin begins by accepting the foolishness of the characters' quest. He says:

Age softens the sense of defeat
As well as the will to success,
. . . .
. . . so now in the mornings
I wake, neither warned nor refreshed,
From dreams without daring, a series
Of vaguely disquieting adventures
Which never end in horror,
Grief or forgiving embraces.

He is dulled into believing that in this life on earth there is meaning only in the sense that there is no meaning. We do not learn from the past, and the future merely depresses, "For vision and longer view / Agree in predicting a day / Of convulsion and vast evil." The present moment we discard, crying, "Miserable wicked me, / How interesting I am." Indeed,

We would rather die in our dread
Than climb the cross of the moment
And let our illusions die.

At the core of this despair in man's ineptitude is the knowledge that we know nothing: "We're quite in the dark." There is one way out, but it is that of which we are most ignorant. Man tries to use reason to find the connection between his life in time ("The clock we are bound to obey") and his hope that his life will not end ("the miracle we must not despair of"), but this "secret" belongs to neither reason nor imagination; it's "too obvious and near to notice" and is "reserved / For the eyes of faith to find."

At this point in Malin's thought, his subway train comes out from underground onto the Manhattan Bridge. The sun has risen, it is day. Malin wraps up the thoughts and activities of the night.

What all the characters had set out to do was to escape the world as it is, to find some safe truth or "lost dad" or "colossal father" who would say: "It's all right, don't worry." Instead they found only worse horrors, more falseness, and finally the world again, unchanged, its ugliness merely intensified. Malin says:

> For the others, like me, there is only the flash
> Of negative knowledge, the night when, drunk, one
> Staggers to the bathroom and stares in the glass
> To meet one's madness. . . .

It would seem to be our very humanity which causes our distress, our refusal to admit that "We belong to our kind, / Are judged as we judge." For in trying to escape time and space, we do not realize that both of them constantly "respond in our own / Contradictory dialect." Everything is, in short, our fault and not our fault. As Malin says in the concluding passage of *The Age of Anxiety*, we are

> . . . unwilling to say yes
> To the Self-So which is the same at all times,
> That Always-Opposite which is the whole subject
> Of our not-knowing. . . . .
> . . . .
> . . . In our anguish we struggle
> To elude Him, to lie to Him, yet His love observes
> His appalling promise. . . . .
> . . . .
> His question disqualifies our quick senses,
> His Truth makes our theories historical sins,
> It is where we are wounded that is when He speaks
> Our creaturely cry, concluding His children
> In their mad unbelief to have mercy on them all
> As they wait unawares for His World to come.

He, of course, is Christ, and Malin's waiting unawares is a far cry from Rosetta's recognition of the need to take the hands of her "poor fat father." We are

back with the narrator of *For the Time Being* or with
Caliban in *The Sea and the Mirror* as Malin, no longer
satanic but sadly priest-like, offers salvation but not
happiness. For here and now there is nothing we can
do. Malin returns to duty, "reclaimed by the actual
world where time is real and in which, therefore, poetry can take no interest." He has done nothing but
articulate, as did Caliban and the Narrator before him,
the feeling that since this life is so miserable there must
be another. Yet there is nothing we can do to reach it
except "sit tight," go on existing, running throughout
our lives, finding some small solace in the recognition
that since there is a "Self-So," there must also be an
"Always-Opposite" or—as Caliban would say—a
"Wholly Other."

In comparison with the tightly knit structure of *The
Sea and the Mirror* or even *For the Time Being*, *The
Age of Anxiety* seems to be a work without movement
or purpose. The things that *do* happen in *The Age of
Anxiety* are mitigated by the fact that the characters do
not really grow. One has the feeling that the "moments
of truth" experienced by Rosetta and Malin have happened before and will happen again, as of course they
have and will. This is Auden's point in *The Age of Anxiety*. He wants to give a picture of the modern world in
action, and to show through the futile, repetitive action
of his characters the futility of man's attempts either to
escape or to resolve the problems of this world. At the
same time, as in both *The Sea and the Mirror* and *For
the Time Being*, Auden feels obliged to offer an even-
tual way out: the recognition of the existence of the
Divine as a presence and a world separate from oneself
and this world. This attempt, which works so well in
the Caliban/Ariel relationship in *The Sea and the
Mirror*, and somewhat less well in the Simeon/Herod
justaposition in *For the Time Being*, seems to fail completely in *The Age of Anxiety*. Perhaps this is because
Auden stacks the deck against his characters. Malin,

who articulates "the message," is unable to make use of what he says. He is damned to the point where not only can he not act, but after speaking he must return to his normal life to forget, until the next drunken evening, what he has thought and said. This process is not the one described by the Narrator of *For the Time Being* when he discusses the manner in which we forget Christ save when reminded of Him at Christmas and at Easter; what happens to Malin is not induced by experiencing either the Incarnation or its reenactment, Malin, through the artificial heightening of his anxiety by drink, has felt the emptiness of his life more strongly than he normally does and so, as a consequence, becomes religious. But, as he himself so deliberately points out, what he feels is only "the flash / Of negative knowledge." He disgusts himself and knows what he is not rather than what he is. His religion is a momentary feeling of necessity, not a permanent change of heart or direction as Caliban's is. He is not a priest, but he is not an antipriest either; he is simply a lost, befuddled man, able to bear living as long as he does not think. He is the type of Christian who falls back on faith as the need arises, but never sees it as a way of life.

Malin is the "voice" of *The Age of Anxiety*. Through him, more than through any other character, Auden speaks. What Malin says is important. It is important to recognize Christ, to recognize that "He speaks / Our creaturely cry." But it is more important to do something with this recognition. Momentary conversion while drunk means nothing, the guilt of the hangover vitiates all. To Auden, Malin is *not* a good man. His despair, his feeling of ineptitude render him impotent, incapable of genuine commitment. He lives in the dark, "too blind or too bored" to really advance.

Yet perhaps the failure of Malin is necessary to compensate for the success of Caliban, for in *The Age of Anxiety* Auden is trying, once and for all, to get rid of the minister/teacher persona of his earlier poems.

More like Tennyson now than Shelley, he wants to make clear the feeling he has that no one knows precisely what life, or afterlife, is all about; that there is no such thing as knowledge, that there is such a thing as faith. In order to do this, he shows us his "old" reason foundering on the rocks. The characters he gives us are modern human beings looking at the abyss and stumbling back into ordinary, frustrated lives. They are all variations on "Auden of the thirties." They search, they grope, until one—Malin—chances upon the Truth. There is, as yet, no Way or Life. These Auden gives us later.

V

The Later Poems

In *The Age of Anxiety* Auden brought the ideas of *The Sea and the Mirror* and *For the Time Being* to a final, pessimistic position: hope for mankind (represented by the characters) in this world is thoroughly destroyed. He gave a dramatic picture of the death of the belief in the possibility of man's self-redemption or even self-improvement, and showed that man—when dependent solely upon his own resources—was not only doomed to failure but damned as well. The only possible note of hope came from Christian faith as Malin perceived it, but Malin could do nothing positive, could not even conceive of positive action. He simply felt that with life as bad as it is, there must be something to keep man from committing suicide, and that something must be the possibility of man's redemption through Christ. Malin's Christ is the true superhero or, as Auden would term Him (if Auden did not believe so devoutly in Him), the true religious hero. Christ is the savior the characters were asking for in "The Dirge," who comes not to "save" society as it is but to help man escape from society's doom. All this Malin realizes, but this realization does nothing to change his life, to "redeem the Time Being from insignificance." He merely goes on with (or rather back to) his ordinary life.

The mood of *The Age of Anxiety* is, finally, one of despair. It is neither a celebration of God's mystery (as was *The Sea and the Mirror*), nor of His presence (as was *For the Time Being*), but simply a picture of mankind's corruption. It is a bitter poem, empty of hope, harsh and strident in technique.

The poems of *Nones* (1951) exhibit a completely different mood. In reading them, one feels that Auden has written himself out of despair and into a benign acceptance of "the Time Being," that he has experienced another "change of heart."

For example, in the second poem, "In Praise of Limestone," Auden employs two devices which one encounters with increasing frequency in the later poems: the gentle, "ordinary" persona and the unidentified other, usually addressed as "dear" or "my dear." In a sense, "In Praise of Limestone" may be seen as a prelude to the "Bucolics" of *The Shield of Achilles*, but it is far superior to any of them.

The persona opens the poem on a tentative, general note, saying,

If it forms the one landscape that we the inconstant
     ones
   Are consistently homesick for, this is chiefly
Because it dissolves in water.[1]

All of the important elements of the poem are introduced in these first three lines. The hesitant note, sounded by "If," continues throughout. Man knows no more in this poem than he did in *The Age of Anxiety, The Sea and the Mirror, For the Time Being,* or any of the earlier poems—he is not even sure that limestone *is* the landscape for which he yearns. But *if* it is, it is "chiefly / Because it dissolves in water." Like man, the limestone has no permanence; contrary to Rosetta's dream landscape or Miranda's childlike vision of her world, the limestone will not sit "always by the sea." The narrator makes no attempt to separate himself from mankind. He is ordinary, one of "the inconstant ones" whose only constancy may be a homesickness for

[1] Auden, *Nones*, p. 13.

a landscape which erodes as they do. Moreover, the landscape is one in which man may dream of accomplishing his goals. It is a "region / Of short distances and definite places," where man's desires to convert, for instance, "a wild to a formal vineyard" can be interpreted as

. . . ingenious but short steps that a child's wish
To receive more attention than his brothers, whether
By pleasing or teasing, can easily take.

From a sentimental point of view, the landscape could be England ("What could be more like Mother . . . ?"), and the child Auden. Yet, in addition to the aspect of the landscape as the home of idealized youth, it is a formal garden as well; its denizens are statues, "modification of matter into / Innocent athletes and gesticulating fountains." There is, as Stephen Spender points out, a suggestion of the castle and gardens of Ischia, an island off Naples where Auden began spending his springs and summers during the time of the composition of the *Nones* poems.[2] Although formed of volcanic rock rather than limestone, Ischia is small in size and dominated by its castle and formal gardens. Or, in a third and historical sense, the landscape could be Greece, with "Mother" as the Earth Mother and man in history the theme.[3] But whether the original inspiration was England, Ischia, or Greece, or a combination of the three, the landscape of the poem is small, island-like, and formalized. It seems the landscape of a work of art, very close, in fact, to that of Keats' "Ode on a

[2] "The island of Ischia, near Naples, enters a good deal into these poems." (Stephen Spender, "Seriously Unserious" [a review of *Nones* by W. H. Auden], *Poetry*, LXXVIII, 6 [September 1951], 352–356.
[3] The scene may very well be an idealization of all three. As Auden says in his essay "Reading" (*The Dyer's Hand*, p. 6), his notion of the Edenesque landscape is one of "Limestone uplands like the Pennines plus a small region of igneous rocks with at least one extinct volcano. A precipitous and indented sea-coast."

Grecian Urn." Take, for example, the opening of the second stanza:

Watch, then, the band of rivals as they climb up and
    down
  Their steep stone gennels in twos and threes, some-
    times
Arm in arm, but never, thank God, in step. . . .

Living men or figures in a work of art, these "rivals" are ordinary men; they know "each other too well to think / There are any important secrets," and "when one of them goes to the bad, the way his mind works / Remains comprehensible." There is no surprise in this limestone landscape; it is an unexceptional world inhabited by unanxious creatures about whom Auden says: "That is why, I suppose, / The best and the worst never stayed here long but sought / Immoderate soils." The "best and worst," the exceptional as opposed to the ordinary, are drawn to the "granite wastes" of would-be sainthood, or, in the case of "Intendant Caesars," to the "clays and gravels" and, for the "really reckless," the "older colder voice" of the ocean. This is familiar Auden territory, with the various hells siphoning off the saintly and the bedeviled, leaving the ordinary pursuing ordinary lives in an ordinary world. Yet all men hear the voices—the "granite wastes," "clays and gravels," and ocean—proving that "this land is not the sweet home that it looks," not "the historical calm of a site / Where something was settled once and for all." On the contrary, "it disturbs our rights."

The limestone landscape makes man aware of time, aware that he has "to look forward / To death as a fact." The "granite wastes" or the ocean may offer the illusion of an escape from time, but this world does not.

This poem presents a much different picture of modern life from that in *The Age of Anxiety*. Although there is still no certitude, and man is still regarded as weak and ignorant—caught in a history he cannot conquer—there is no feeling of hatred or contempt; instead, there is a soft and sympathetic understanding. As Stephen Spender says, " 'In Praise of Limestone' is a didactic poem which reaches far beyond the didactic. Instead of being a personal poem with a moral, it is a morality which reveals a person." [4]

The "person" Spender speaks of is Auden's new persona. The didacticism of Auden's earlier poems demanded that the persona be both pupil and teacher. The emotional content of these poems (whether it was the hope of "Petition," the feeling of impotence of "September 1, 1939," or the horror and futility of *The Age of Anxiety*) came from Auden's original belief that man could and would be taught. Consequently, the "voices" of the poems were continually preaching, either with the hope of success or the bitterness of failure. As has been noted earlier, with the failure of Malin to employ constructively his considerable knowledge, in *The Age of Anxiety* Auden hoped to ring a death knell for the preacher/teacher as a meaningful voice. When Malin goes back home to prepare for the next day, he is unchanged, merely one of the "beasts who repeat themselves."

The "voice" of "In Praise of Limestone" is neither preacher nor teacher. He is simply there. Caliban, of course, was "there" too, downstage with the rest of us, but he was a leader. The persona of "In Praise of Limestone" does not try to lead. He merely observes what is around him and does not even really judge.

This understanding and acceptance are maintained throughout the poems of *Nones*. Many of the poems are really just light verse or occasional poems, such as "Serenade," "The Love Feast," and "Under Which Lyre." However, there are several longer, more serious works included in this collection, and, among these,

[4] Spender, "Seriously Unserious," p. 355.

"Ischia," dedicated to Brian Howard, is perhaps the most positive poem in the volume.

In this poem, Auden commemorates the island in all its aspects, from its fishing ports to its hot springs. Even though he knows "that all is never well," he is able to accept this limitation since "Nothing is free." Yet Auden does not tell us what the payment shall be. He merely says, "whatever you charge shall be paid," leav- the light and happy tone of the poem intact. "Ischia" serves as an indication of poems to come, for although richer than the light verse of "Serenade," it is still no more than a celebratory poem, a "bless what there is for being" poem like those of *About The House.* But we are not yet firmly and comfortably within that house. Unable to know, able to praise, Auden's persona is also still able to imagine fear, to hear a voice

> Ask as one might the time or a trifle
> Extra her money and her life.

These two lines conclude "Pleasure Island," the poem which follows "Ischia" in *Nones.* Like the Pleasure Is- land of Pinochio, this island offers the senses all of the irresistible pleasures they could desire, and to Auden, at this stage, any pleasure that is irresistible is also cor- ruptible. The relationship between "Ischia" and "Plea- sure Island" is an interesting one. In "Ischia" Auden is straightforward and celebratory, talking about a real place that means a great deal to him. In "Pleasure Is- land" he mixes sensuality and moral admonishment, yet he is really talking about the same place in both poems. Pleasure Island is Ischia fictionalized, and Miss Lovely the persona characterized. Looking at these two poems as two sides of the same coin, we receive a fairly clear picture of Auden's stance at this time. If, as the persona of "In Praise of Limestone" seems to believe, one is really unable to know anything, if there is no certitude possible, then what does man do without answers to

113

his questions? For one, he stops questioning. For another, he simply looks at the world around him with accepting, appreciative eyes. This world is Ischia, and the poem "Ischia" is Auden's testimony to his acceptance of its beauty. Yet there is a danger in this acceptance and appreciation of beauty. It is the danger, as Caliban warned, of becoming a debauchee. If one accepts, one may be tempted to give oneself over to the senses. And, if one succumbs, the price he will have to pay is that paid by Miss Lovely: a dark night of the soul in which he, like Hopkins' wretch of "Carrion Comfort," lies "wrestling with (my God!) my God."

It is this fear of confrontation with his god that keeps Auden and his persona aware of the Pleasure Island nascent in Ischia, and, as a result, his acceptance and appreciation of sensual beauty are controlled.

It is interesting to note that here, in *Nones*, Auden felt it necessary to present one last warning of the dangers inherent in the new attitude he was assuming. By the time we reach the pure celebratory verse of *About the House*, there no longer seems to be a need to warn, merely a need to praise. But in *Nones*, Auden is deadly serious about the price that man must eventually pay for his life and the way he lives it. There is no joke when man confronts God.

Two more poems in *Nones* deserve special consideration because the contrast between them gives very clear evidence of the "old" and "new" Auden. The first of these, "Memorial for the City," is a long and complicated poem. For an epigraph Auden uses a quotation from Juliana of Norwich: "In the self-same point that our soul is made sensual, in the self-same point is the City of God ordained to him from without beginning." The poem itself is in apposition to the epigraph, for it gives us a picture of what has happened to man throughout history as he attempts to avoid the confrontation, as he attempts to build the City of Man instead of facing the City of God. In the poem, Auden analyzes the City of Man. The first section is dominated by "The eyes of the crow and the eye of the camera." They are the eyes of earth, "the abiding / Mother of gods and men," and they "Record a space where time has no place." In the world seen by these eyes, nature is firmly in control; human life goes on, but seemingly with neither purpose nor progress, repeating itself in a world where crime appears to be man's failure to redeem time or God's failure to offer reasons for the loss of time. But Auden says that the eyes lie, that "The crime of life is not time," and that although life seems unbearable, "We are not to despair." For Auden Christ's life changed everything, offering salvation instead of the dead end of death; "Our grief is not Greek," and "We know without knowing there is reason for what we hear." At least we know "that our hurt is not a desertion," and that the chief crime we could commit would be to pity either ourselves or our city.

Yet the city is destroyed, it becomes a rubble dominated by crows, cameras, searchlights, and loudspeakers. In the second section of the poem, Auden documents its decline and fall. From the "New City" of the first stanza to the "abolished City," which appears in the third section and which is the result of the collaborative efforts of man and time, Auden carefully plots the havoc man wreaks through ideas. The "New City" rose from the opposition between Pope Gregory and the Emperor, "the yes and no / Of a rival allegiance"; in this city facts and acts bore a double meaning, "Limbs became hymns; embraces expressed in jest / A more permanent tie." Then came the "Sane City" where "disciplined logicians fought to recover thought / From the eccentricities of the private brain." From this came the "Sinful City," followed by Luther "in a sandy province," who denounced both the "Sinful City" and the church as "obscene." Thereafter, through the processes of time, came "the drums of a clear idea, / The aim of the Rational City"; "the fear or the pride of the Glittering City"; and finally the "Conscious City" whose residents died "Faithful without faith."

In the third section of the poem, the scene is the "abolished City," where,

> Behind the wire
> Which is behind the mirror, Our Image is the same
> Awake or dreaming. . . .

This image is of mankind, or the nature of man; "It can be counted, multiplied, employed," and we are tempted to ask, as did Quant of his image in *The Age of Anxiety*, "Is it our friend?" The answer is no—it is not our friend; it is us. Auden says,

> This is the flesh we are but never would believe,
> The flesh we die but it is death to pity;
> This is Adam waiting for His City.

Man cannot quit. He falls from Grace, he destroys his city, and yet beyond the horror and the barbed wire he waits patiently to fall and destroy again. It is man's nature Auden turns to when he says, concluding section three and introducing section four, "Let Our Weakness Speak." The voice of "Our Weakness" is the voice of man as he is, composed of both spirit and flesh. It is the voice of human life. Yet man will not accept the condition of his existence. He tries to understand, or escape, or destroy, and in each of his attempts he sins. He grasps for either flesh or spirit, wishing to simplify or clarify his life, and in so doing merely muddles it. Why, asks Auden in this poem, can man not realize that Christ's Fifth Word from the cross was directed to him? "I thirst," said Christ, and in so saying pointed out that although He was Spirit—soon to join the Father—He was still Flesh, God become man. In Christ, the abyss, the "grinning gap" had been crossed. The voice of "Our Weakness" understands this and feels disgusted by the repeated delusions of history, by man's foolish attempts to build the "too-great city." Man, it would seem, will never learn that in his "Weakness," his humanity, he holds all the knowledge he can hope to gain in this world.

"Memorial for the City" fails as a poem because the spirit behind it is not really Auden's. Once it was, in "New Year Letter" or in the shorter poems of the thirties, but the spirit, as well as the voice, was laid to rest in the chaos of *The Age of Anxiety.* The problem with "Memorial for the City" is that Auden already knows the message of "Our Weakness," has accepted it, and has told us so. As a result, "Memorial for the City" seems strident, pretentious, and hollow. Yet the poem has interest because it gives further evidence that Auden has not quite reached the point, in *Nones,* where he is content to just sit back with this message he has accepted and talk about it. "Memorial for the City" is one last, stuttering cry from the "old" Auden.

A much different poem is the next to the last of the volume, "Precious Five." It reiterates the "message" of "Memorial for the City" without the awkward allusions and strident tone. It seems to be a direct, modern copy of Hopkins' "The Habit of Perfection." [5] The poem is composed of six stanzas, one directed to each of the senses and one to all five together. Its tone is light, and the poem depends more upon rhyme to carry it than does any other poem in the volume; yet its intent is serious.

Auden singles out each of the senses by directing it to its particular worldly duty, even though it does not know why it should fulfill it. To all five he says, "Be happy, precious five, / So long as I'm alive," giving them the same advice that he, were he to angrily "face the sky and roar," would himself receive: *"Bless what there is for being."* This "Bless what there is for being"

5 *Poems of Gerard Manley Hopkins,* ed. W. H. Gardner (New York: Oxford University Press, 1948), p. 46.

hovers over Auden's poetry throughout the 1950s and 1960s, just as "a change of heart" hovered over his works of the 1930s. Instead of allowing his appreciation of the world of the senses to corrupt him by giving in to it, man blesses what is, informing sensual experience with religious meaning. Here is the control Auden was concerned about in "Ischia" and "Pleasure Island"; by blessing the world, man prevents the "dark night" confrontation with God and keeps himself, hopefully, at a safe distance from both his anxiety and his world.

In the poems comprising *Nones*, Auden gives evidence that he is working on a new persona. The pre-Second World War persona of the angry young Marxist–Freudian was destroyed both by Auden's horror at the atrocities of which he saw man to be capable and by his (maybe resultant) reconversion to orthodox Christianity. While Auden was losing the "mask" of his youth, he turned to dramatic form in which he had long been interested and used it as a transitional device, the result being the three long, dramatic poems of the forties. It is possible, of course, to see variations of the new Auden persona in these poems (in, for example, Caliban and Prospero of *The Sea and the Mirror*, the Narrator of *For the Time Being*, and perhaps in certain aspects of both Quant and Malin of *The Age of Anxiety*), but it is not until *Nones* that this persona really begins to take definite shape, and not until *The Shield of Achilles* does "he" control an entire volume. This new man is benign; he does not curse the ills of the world nor rail at its inadequacies. He accepts his own being and the being of the world wistfully—he is smiling but sad. He is wise in the ways of the world, but not jaded; he is a gentle, humble man.

For this new face, Auden needs and creates a new landscape. Gone is the psychologically symbolic landscape which exploded violently around the characters of *The Age of Anxiety*; in its stead is the simple, realistic landscape of life in the world as it is. In "In Praise of

Limestone" Auden introduced this new landscape symbolically, and in the first section of *The Shield of Achilles* (1955) he establishes it in realistic terms. Auden calls this section "Bucolics." It consists of seven poems, each of which treats a particular aspect of nature and each of which is dedicated to an acquaintance or friend.

The limestone landscape represented for Auden the scene and conditions of human life, its constant flux and erosion carried on with a "murmur" rather than a bang. In "Streams," the last and happiest of the "Bucolics," we see some of what Auden feels that "murmur" means:

And dearer, water, than ever your voice, as if
Glad—though goodness knows why—to run with the
 human race,
 Wishing, I thought, the least of men their
Figures of splendor, their holy places.[6]

The stream is Auden's favorite aspect of his new landscape. It is "Dear water, clear water." It is both unspoilable and sympathetic, without malice towards man, and Auden sees no reason to fear it. Mountains, his old favorite, are too frightening and lonely for this "new" Auden. As he says:

 . . . For an uncatlike
 Creature who has gone wrong
 Five minutes on even the nicest mountain
 Is awfully long.

In the rest of the "Bucolics" Auden completes his landscape, showing both its good and bad aspects and the type of human appeal that each feature possesses. The overall effect of the seven poems is a presentation

[6] W. H. Auden, *The Shield of Achilles* (New York: Random House, 1955), p. 31.

of not so much a world as a character. Auden wants us to see his new persona wandering through nature, pausing to respond to each aspect. There is no inherent evil or good in any particular aspect, but, as Auden says about the plains, "I've reason to be frightened / Not of plains, of course, but of me." Man sees nature as a mirror of himself, and for Auden's timid, self-conscious, middle-aged persona such things as mountains are frightening because their isolation demands or creates an extraordinary man. It is difficult for an ordinary man to bless them.

The values reflected by nature are really in the eye and imagination of the beholder. Man is the one who feels and chooses, and nature takes on meaning from the man who confronts it. Auden's new landscape is really no different from the old; it is only that man has stopped asking it for answers.

The second section of *The Shield of Achilles,* "In Sunshine and Shade," contains fourteen poems, including the title poem of the volume. These poems vary in length and technique, but they are all comments of one sort or another on social man, man interacting with his fellows. The title poem shows the work of art as a mirror of life. Thetis (as audience or viewer) looks over Hephaestos' shoulder as he paints scenes on the shield he is making for Achilles. What she wants to see is the world of Homer with its landscapes, battles, and games idealized. What she actually sees is a series of pictures at the other extreme. The modern shield is as ultrareal as the ancient one seems ultraromantic. Instead of the ancient world idealized, the modern Thetis sees the present world denuded of any illusion of beauty or goodness, a world where every expectation is met with a cruel reversal, where a Sermon on the Mount is composed of statistics and a desire for "ritual pieties" is fulfilled by the Crucifixion. The third and last of these reversals is worth examining in detail. Thetis has expected to see a celebration of "athletes at their games" or a scene of "Men and women in a dance"; what she sees instead is a picture in which

> A ragged urchin, aimless and alone,
> Loitered about that vacancy; a bird
> Flew up to safety from his well-aimed stone.

The world this boy knows is one of rape, knifings, and other violence. It is the world without Christianity, in which the boy has

> . . . never heard
> Of any world where promises were kept
> Or one could weep because another wept.

The whole structure of "The Shield of Achilles" seems to be based on the premise that without Christianity the romance of the Homeric legend would be translated and transformed into the inhuman ugliness of the contemporary world. The shield of legend when looked at in reality, outside the guise of art, would reveal the world as it is, which, when viewed without the compassionate perspective of Christianity, is an arid, inhospitable, lonely place. It is only with Christianity and the idea of the coinherence that the "ragged urchin" could be shown a world where "one could weep because another wept." "Shield" is similar to "Memorial for the City" in that it is basically a warning poem, but it succeeds where the other fails because the warning is presented in controlled nondidactic images. The "ragged urchin" has no grief, not even Greek, and if we do, or do not, Auden does not feel he has to spell it out for us. Auden has become more sure of his new attitude, and the shrillness of tone heard in some of the poems of *Nones* is gone from his voice. He is able here, and with even greater effect in "Horae Canonicae," to

let his images speak for themselves and to let the reader
see the meaning in their interaction for himself. It is up
to us to see Christ in Auden's new world.

The other poems in this section make varying comments in various tones on man's social problems. "Fleet
Visit," for instance, which follows "The Shield of Achilles," gives a picture of sailors landing in a foreign port
in peacetime; as Auden says, "They are not here because / But only just-in-case." They are innocent, mild-
looking boys, not in the least heroic; in fact "One base-
ball game is more / To them than fifty Troys." Yet in
spite of (or perhaps because of) their innocence they
are a bit lost, for, unlike "The whore and ne'er-do-well /
Who pester them with junk," they have no social function; with no war they have no role. This is one of the
greatest human problems, at least to Auden's mind: the
human being is unable, save in death, to be in repose.
He must be doing—if not creating, then destroying.
The ships in the harbor, on the other hand, "actually
gain / From having nothing to do": ships are free just to
exist aesthetically, but man, unfortunately, has what he
feels to be moral and social obligations to fulfill.

"Ode to Gaea" shows man viewing the world from
the vantage point of an airplane.[7] In "The Shield of

---

[7] Auden writes in "Hic et Ille" (*The Dyer's Hand*, p. 101):

From the height of 10,000 feet, the earth appears to the human
eye as it appears to the eye of a camera; that is to say, all
history is reduced to nature. This has the salutary effect of
making historical evils, like national divisions and political
hatreds, seem absurd. I look down from an airplane upon a
stretch of land which is obviously continuous. That, across it,
marked by a tiny ridge or river or even by no topographical
sign whatever, there should run a frontier, and that the human
beings living on one side should hate or refuse to trade with
or be forbidden to visit those on the other side, is instantaneously
revealed to me as ridiculous. Unfortunately, I cannot have
this revelation without simultaneously having the illusion that
there are no historical values either. From the same height I
cannot distinguish between an outcrop of rock and a Gothic
cathedral, or between a happy family playing in a backyard
and a flock of sheep, so that I am unable to feel any difference
between dropping a bomb upon one or the other. If the effect

Achilles" Thetis was dismayed that art did not give her what she wanted—glamour, romance, escape—but gave instead an exaggeration of the harshness of reality. She was demanding a lie but got the truth. In "Ode to Gaea," the persona looks down at earth and wonders what he can do to fit in.

Earth, from the perspective of the air (far-removed), is gigantic, mysterious, and almost unapproachable. Man, historically and individually, seems miniscule. Earth is "the real one," and to her all man's attempts to build cities or civilizations (to make "good land-scapes") seem "but lies" or vain, naïve dreams. The natural world is not the place for the lion to lie down with the lamb. Earth has no morality in the sense that man conceives of it; rather, if she were forced to make a value judgment she would feel that "Of pure things Water is the best!" This is not reality as man wants to think of it because it is a reality uninformed by morality, a reality unimpressed by man's feelings of self-importance in the natural scheme of things. Yet it exists and therefore is worth praise. As Auden said in "Precious Five," *"Bless what there is for being,"* and "Earth, till the end, will be herself." And, even if man does not like it, there is nothing he can do about it. But, if Earth does not change, man does, or at least should.

In the last section of *The Shield of Achilles,* "Horae Canonicae," Auden gives us a picture of man in time. "Horae Canonicae" consists of seven poems, one for each of the canonical hours and offices, beginning with Prime and concluding with Lauds. Within this framework Auden creates his most complicated work since *The Age of Anxiety.*

As Auden celebrated the Nativity in *For the Time Being,* he now, in "Horae Canonicae," celebrates the

of distance upon the observed and the observer were mutual, so that, as the objects on the group shrank in size and lost their uniqueness, the observer in the airplane felt himself shrinking and becoming more and more generalized, we should either give up flying as too painful or create a heaven on earth.

Crucifixion, the supreme substitution, demonstrating that although the historical Christ was only crucified once, men throughout the ages rekill him symbolically each day. In fact, Auden uses the Crucifixion as an event to show the fact of death to all men: as Christ died so must we all. In the death of another, and particularly in a sacrificial death such as the Crucifixion, we feel that we as individuals are eluding death. Of course this is not true, for death is not eluded, merely postponed. Christ's death did not offer an escape from death, it offered us the possibility of following "the Way." What Auden asks is that we recognize the fact of death and then use this recognition in living. In order to ask this, Auden takes us step by step, hour by hour, through the day.

"Prime" (6 A.M.) begins the sequence and the day as

> Simultaneously, as soundlessly,
> Spontaneously, suddenly,
> . . . .
> . . . the gates of the mind,
> The horn gate and the ivory gate,
> Swing to, swing shut, instanteously,

and man (the persona here represents every man) slides sibilantly into consciousness: "Without a name or history I wake / Between my body and the day." Each day begins, like human history, with the creation, with "The Adam sinless in our beginning / Adam still previous to any act." This is the state of innocence, and man has yet to become self-conscious, to Fall, and to be man. But, for each man in each day, as for original Adam, paradise is "Lost of course," and man becomes aware of the distinction between himself and the world he sees.

By 9 A.M. ("Terce"), man is deeply involved in the split between his public and his private self. The hangman shakes paws with his dog before going to find out "who will be provided / To do the high works of Justice with." The judge gently closes the door for his headache-ridden wife before setting out "to apply on earth the Law that rules the stars." The poet takes a "breather / Round his garden" before writing a Truth he does not yet know. So it is that every man "Prays to an image of his image of himself" that he may get through the day without pain and with, perhaps, a little pleasure. The members of mankind are interchangeable ("At this hour we all might be anyone"); all of them share the same human hopes and doubts. It is only the victim "who is without a wish," for the victim knows that he is the one who will die, "that by sundown / We shall have had a good Friday." He knows that there will be no miracle save that of his death, that all our small prayers are heard, "That the machinery of our world will function / Without a hitch." This knowledge is, to the persona and (by extention) to all mankind, what is unforgivable; it is the essence of the victim's crime. For, "If he knows the answers, / Then why are we here, why is there even dust?" Why, in other words, must we continue searching? Why do we not have heaven?

"Sext" (noon) describes the characters involved in the Crucifixion: the executioner, the authorities, and the crowd. The executioner is the man with a vocation, the man capable of forgetting himself when performing a function. As with a fine cook, surgeon, or clerk, "you have only to watch his eyes," for all of these men share "the same rapt expression, . . . that eye-on-the-object look." These functionaries make civilization possible, for without their simple dedication to the job at hand we would be without our city.

If eyes identify the serious workers, mouths give the clue to those in authority. Auden calls these mouths "judicial" and feels that they "belong for the most part / to very great scoundrels." Through the power of their self-righteousness, they have given to mankind "basilicas, divas, / dictionaries, pastoral verse, / the courtesies of the city," and the authority "at this noon . . . / to command this death."

In contrast to the men of toil and those of decisive action is the vacant, characterless, and indispensable crowd, which "rejects no one" because "joining the crowd / Is the only thing all men can do."

"Nones" (3 p.m.) takes us past the time of the Crucifixion to the midafternoon heat and quiet. It is siesta time, and "The day is too hot, too bright, too still, / Too ever, the dead remains too nothing." Moreover, everyone is gone. "The hangman has gone to wash, the soldiers to eat," and even the crowd ("The faceless many who always / Collect when any world is to be wrecked") has dispersed. Its members "Lie sprawled now, calmly sleeping, / Harmless as sheep"; any one of them, if questioned, would reply, "It was a monster with one red eye, / A crowd that saw him die, not I." We are the only ones left—"We are left alone with our feat." So begins the recognition of individual guilt. Left alone as individuals, we are confronted by the act completed, "we are surprised / At the ease and speed of our deed / And uneasy." There is no ignoring or escaping it, for from the moment of the Crucifixion on through time "wherever / The sun shines, brooks run, books are written, / There will also be this death," that fact which "The mutilated flesh, our victim, / Explains too nakedly, too well."

In *For the Time Being* Auden presented us with the problem of what man was to do once he had experienced the Incarnation and yet was forced to live without Christ, once he believed in the reality of heaven and yet remained separate from it. Man was asked to try to find ways in which to redeem "the Time Being" from insignificance. In "Nones," the pivotal poem in "Horae Canonicae," Auden gives us man confronted by the communal and individual guilt and responsibility for the Crucifixion. In Auden's thought, this is the logical extension of the import of *For the Time Being:* given the possibility of eternity, man is bound to try to destroy it, and, once having succeeded, man is bound to recognize what he has done and to try to find an escape. Yet, no matter how hard man tries, he cannot escape the meaning of the death, and ultimately each man pays with his own life.

Meanwhile, waiting to make that payment, man must do something; it is the problem once again of "the Time Being." Sleep, taking consciousness away from "our own wronged flesh," gives us the chance to help nature keep us alive, "restoring / The order we try to destroy." The relief from guilt and responsibility afforded by sleep places our bodies back in the innocence of nature where, not understanding and yet not bothered by our inability to understand, we are able to be "awed / By death" like the animals. In short, we are aware and involved (as all living beings are in death) but not responsible.

"Vespers" (6 P.M.) presents an evening confrontation between the persona and his opposite. There is no conversation, merely an exchange of looks as "with a passing glance we take the other's posture." This glance, however, is enough, for "Both simultaneously recognise his Anti-type: that I am an Arcadian, that he is a Utopian." They also recognize that "between my Eden and his New Jerusalem, no treaty is negotiable." Besides this recognition and a catalogue of reasons as to why contact between them is not possible, the meeting is

> . . . also a rendezvous between accomplices who,
>   in spite of themselves,
> cannot resist meeting

> to remind the other (do both, at bottom, desire
>   truth?) of that half of
> their secret which he would most like to forget,

> forcing us both, for a fraction of a second, to remember our victim

(but for him I could forget the blood, but for me he
        could forget the
innocence)

        on whose immolation (call him Abel, Remus, whom
                you will, it is one
Sin Offering) arcadias, utopias, our dear old bag of a
                democracy, are alike
founded:

        For without a cement of blood (it must be human,
                it must be innocent)
no secular wall will safely stand.

The recognition of one's opposite necessarily entails
recognition of one's self as well as of one's place as a
social being.[8] This is because it is possible, when alone,
to believe oneself to be outside society and perhaps
outside of time and history as well. But in the act of
confronting one's opposite comes an awareness of the
common element of humanity, of a common bond one

[8] Auden, in "Hic et Ille" (*The Dyer's Hand*, p. 106), describes:
Two cyclic madmen. In his elated phase, A feels: "I am God.
The universe is full of gods. I adore and am adored by all."
B feels: "The universe is only a thing. I am happily free from
all bonds of attachment to it." In the corresponding depressed
phase, A feels: "I am a devil. The universe is full of devils. I
hate all and am hated by all." B feels: "I am only a thing to
the universe which takes no interest in me." This difference is
reflected in their behavior. When elated A does not wash and
even revels in dirt because all things are holy. He runs after
women, after whores in particular whom he intends to save
through Love. But B in this mood takes a fastidious pride in
his physical cleanliness as a mark of his superiority and is
chaste for the same reason. When depressed A begins to wash
excessively to cleanse himself from guilt and feels a morbid
horror of all sex. B now neglects his appearance because "nobody cares how I look," and tries to be a Don Juan seducer
in an attempt to compel life to take an interest in him.
A's God—Zeus–Jehovah; B's God—The Unmoved Mover. Thus
Auden depicts one way in which opposites with conflicting attitudes
can be led, through their own dialectics, into similar patterns of
social excess and muddled self-understanding.

shares with all mankind and also with one's own past. In his "Anti-type" the persona meets the voice of the "old" Auden of "Petition," and, although the "old" and "new" Auden do not like each other, they must, like Caliban and Ariel, recognize each other's existence.[9]

"Compline" (9 P.M.) brings the day to its close. Man is about to sleep, to let his body join the "Plants in their chaster peace which is more / To its real taste." At this time of day man would like to put things together in a coherent "instant of recollection / When the whole thing makes sense." But this is impossible. When the persona tries, he finds only "Actions, words, that could fit any tale." He finds neither plot nor meaning save for the peculiar fact that he "cannot remember / A thing between noon and three." At the end of the day there is no fulfillment; only the recognition of lack of knowledge or, perhaps, a disguised evasion of guilt. Maybe the heart, by purely existing and functioning, knows what the stars know. Maybe not. All the conscious persona knows is that "I neither know what they know/ Nor what I ought to know." As he begins to sink from consciousness into sleep and into the vague fancies and wishes of dreams, and finally into nothing, the persona is placed in a dilemma: will he, like the day that has passed, pass into history and exist only as a fact of the past? The alternative is a difficult tone to accept. As he says, "It is not easy / To believe in unknowable justice / Or pray in the name of a love / Whose name one's forgotten." And yet, that seems preferable to the dead end of nothing, so the persona prays:

> . . . spare
> Us in the youngest day when all are

[9] Auden says elsewhere of this need, in "A Knight of the Infinite" (a review of *Gerard Manley Hopkins: A Life* by Eleanor Ruggles), *The New Republic*, August 21, 1944, p. 223: "There are two external classes of men, the Knight and the Bourgeois, Don Quixote and Sancho Panza, Holmes and Watson, Pascal and Montaigne, the man who is capable of excess, and the man who is not. Each needs the other."

Shaken awake, facts are facts
(And I shall know exactly what happened
Today between noon and three)
That we, too, may come to the picnic
With nothing to hide, join the dance
As it moves in perichoresis,
Turns about the abiding tree.

If, in looking at this prayer, we think back to "Petition," we get a good idea of the road Auden has travelled and is travelling. No longer is it just the suicides ("will its negative inversion") who are unforgiven, it is all of us, the living and the dead. And there is no "Sir" to "look shining" at us; instead there is our earnest plea, "spare / Us." The god (if god he was) of "Petition" served as a guide or an approving helpmate, but the god in this prayer is God, and although he does not help, he may spare. This is the "new" Auden, asking not for guidance, but for mercy.

"Lauds" completes the cycle with a vision of the new dawn. The world is now Christian, since man has taken that hesitant step into belief. As "The crow of the cock commands awakening; / Already the mass-bell goes dong-ding." The world is saved and life goes on, but with some differences. No longer is man alone, as he was in the awakening of "Prime," for now "Men of their neighbors become sensible," and the prayer is not only "save me" but has become:

God bless the Realm, God bless the People;
God bless this green world temporal:
In solitude, for company.

The search is over. No longer "alone, out over seventy thousand fathoms," Prospero, become the "new" persona, has joined the coinherence and sings not only "In solitude," but "for company."

The "message" of "Horae Canonicae" (and the seven

poems are so interdependent that they should be considered as a whole) might be summarized as follows: Each day of his life each man is faced with a number of decisions (as though each day were the original Good Friday). He must decide to join mankind, maintaining his own essential isolation but nonetheless recognizing his involvement with, and responsibility to, the lives and acts of all other men. This decision is retroactive in its consequences as well, involving him in past events of human history: for instance, how would he have acted had he been present at the Crucifixion? [10] By virtue of his very humanness, there is no reason to suspect he would have acted differently then than now, and this answer to the question reveals more fully than do any of Auden's other poems the nature of Auden's new persona. He is a witness to the act; although he is neither the executioner (see "Sext") nor the authority behind the executioner, he is more than a mere member of the crowd and cannot absolve himself of guilt by blaming it on the group. Perhaps the key to his character is his awareness. Through the body of the poem ("Prime" to "Compline") he is constantly developing, trying to understand. As is natural to man, he wants answers, wants to make sense out of the relationship between himself and his world. Most of all he wants to recollect and clarify the Crucifixion. The position he arrives at is that there is no reason either in the world or in himself

[10] Auden, in "The Virgin and the Dynamo" (*The Dyer's Hand*, pp. 69–70), says:

(1) A historical world exists, a world of unique events and unique persons, related by analogy, not identity. The number of events and analogical relations is potentially infinite. The existence of such a world is a good, and every addition to the number of events, persons and relations is an additional good.

(2) The historical world is a fallen world, i.e. though it is good that it exists, the way in which it exists is evil, being full of unfreedom and disorder.

(3) The historical world is a redeemable world. The unfreedom and disorder of the past can be reconciled in the future.

that can adequately explain it, and this he is finally able to accept. This development divides the poem into three sections (plus a coda, "Lauds," at the end): the introduction and preparation for the act ("Prime" and "Terce"); the act itself as seen in terms of those around it ("Sext"); and the attempts of the persona to understand it ("Nones," "Vespers," and "Compline"). The third section is itself subdivided into awe at the fact of death, horror at the recognition of responsibility for participation in it, and finally the recognition of the fact that he is unable to understand not only the Crucifixion but life itself. Thus the "story" of "Horae Canonicae" is the story of an individual's conversion to faith brought about through his inability to understand either himself or his fellow man.

It is precisely this inability to understand that leads to the leap of faith of Kierkegaard. Something has happened; someone has died, been crucified. That person was innocent. The persona and those around him still live. Why? Since the Crucifixion, man has pondered the guilt arising from that one particular death. The answer, Auden feels, lies in the simple fact that Christ died for us, to offer us redemption. Man's logic can find no reason for Christ's substitution. It was because God willed it. The act of faith lies in recognizing the fact of the Crucifixion (accepting the idea that something happened "between noon and three" which is beyond man's comprehension), and in accepting the idea of the coinherence which goes along with it. Man no longer needs to know, he needs to love. This is, to Auden, the only possible solution to the incredible paradox of killing a man who dies to save you. Man must believe that he has been given the Way, the Truth, and the Life. Through believing in the seemingly unbelievable, man should be able to look around him and accept himself and his world as both guilty and good.

The power of "Horae Canonicae" lies in the fact that the voice of the poet (his persona) is both actor and viewer; he not only describes the surrounding event but tries to evaluate his own participation in them. The result is a poem of both immediacy and distance, a poem in which the particular and the general are merged.

The Shield of Achilles in its three sections (dealing with nature, man and nature, and man beyond nature) presents as complete a picture of Auden's new position and persona as "New Year Letter" gave of Auden in transition. Auden's two subsequent volumes, *Homage to Clio* and *About the House,* merely expand upon and clarify the attitudes and materials contained in *The Shield of Achilles.*

Homage to Clio (1960) consists of two major sections (titled simply Part I and Part II), with a transitional prose section on the making of a poem and an appendix of a group of clerihews which Auden calls "Academic Graffiti." At first reading there appears to be no visible pattern to the volume, and, in the sense of pattern as seen in *The Shield of Achilles,* there is none. But there is a single interest or point of view which does bring a unity to the collection.

"Horae Canonicae" seems to be, at least at this writing, Auden's final statement on the subject of Christian belief. In contrast to its seriousness, *Homage to Clio* appears comic, if not frivolous, and indeed its poems *are* comic—comic in terms of being all too human. They bear the same relationship to those of the preceding volume as *The Age of Anxiety* bears to *For the Time Being.* The difference between *Homage to Clio* and *The Age of Anxiety* lies in the difference between the "new" Auden with his new persona and the "old" or, more properly, the "transitional" Auden. *The Age of Anxiety,* as we have seen, gave vent to the last of Auden's disgust and bewilderment with mankind which had supplanted the belief in possible improvement characteristic of his work in the early thirties. In *For the Time Being* Auden presented the possibility for salvation inherent in the Incarnation; in *The Age of*

Anxiety, he presented man's inability to realize it. In "Horae Canonicae" Auden presents man's guilt, his acceptance of it, and the realization that he is still, nonetheless, offered salvation. It settles matters out of historical time and resolves the difficulties man has with God. By the time of the composition of the poems in *Homage to Clio,* Auden has completed his metaphysical examination and is left with the problem of man the individual versus man in historical time. This conflict, then, is the subject matter of the volume.

Although Clio is the goddess of history, the poems are not devoted to her; indeed the emphasis is much more on man than muse. There is no need for Clio to "be represented in granite," for she is always with us as the "Muse of the unique / Historical fact," of the individual human action. The individual, however, need not be great, for Auden's prime concern is, as it was in "Horae Canonicae," with "all poor s-o-b's who never / Do anything properly." Or, as he says in "Makers of History," instead of kings and heroes,

Clio loves those who bred them better horses,
Found answers to their questions, made their things,
Even those fulsome
Bards they boarded. . . .

It is ordinary man who is the subject of *Homage to Clio,* or the ordinary aspects of the great, and all of the poems in *Homage to Clio* echo this idea. Man, no matter what he does or tries to do in life, remains man; the greatest have their failures, the least their successes The tone of the poems is light, as if Auden has finally realized that light verse must not be metaphysical. Even the toughness of rhythm and language of "Dame Kind" is mitigated by such lines as "She mayn't be all she might be but / She *is* our Mum." The acceptance of the reality of living is Auden's concern in *Homage to Clio.* Caliban has stopped trying to be a priest and has decided just to try to live. Or, as the persona says in "Good-bye to the Mezzogiorno," it is best

> To bless this region, its vendages, and those
>   Who call it home: though one cannot always
> Remember exactly why one has been happy,
>   There is no forgetting that one was.

Ahab has accepted the advice of "Our Weakness," and it is this attitude of acceptance that brings man and history together, putting man in the proper perspective regarding time.

About the House (1965) makes use of this new attitude towards life and time in describing man's relationship to his environment, and shows the point towards which Auden has been progressing since the conclusion of *The Age of Anxiety*. There we were shown man lost, caught between God, the immediate world, and history. At the conclusion of "The Seven Stages," the symbolic landscape of Auden's earlier poetry was destroyed by the confrontation of the characters with the real world. There was no escape for them because there is no escape in life. One horrible aspect of reality is the fact that it is real.

The Age of Anxiety is the low point of Auden's poetry. It is a work of despair and, as such, brings to a climax the transitional work of Auden in the early and mid-forties. In the composition of the poems of *Nones*, Auden is literally beginning from scratch. He must develop (and he does) a new attitude towards man, both as an individual and as a member of a group, and the world around him. This he begins to do in *Nones* by sketching the outlines of a new persona, and he furthers it in *The Shield of Achilles* by relating man to nature, God, and his fellow man. With *Homage to Clio* he places man in time and tries to bring together the human aspects of beast and angel. Finally, with *About the House,* he puts his new man into his new home.

About the House is divided into two sections. One is devoted to descriptions of individual rooms, and the other is concerned with travel to different places. The dominant attitude of the entire volume may best be summed up by an excerpt from a poem in the first section called "Thanksgiving for a Habitat" (which lends its name to the entire first section). Auden ends the poem:

> . . . Territory, status,
>
> and love, sing all the birds, are what matter:
>   what I dared not hope or fight for
> is, in my fifties, mine, a toft-and-croft
>   where I needn't, ever, be at home *to*
>
> those I am not at home *with,* not a cradle,
>   a magic Eden without clocks,
> and not a windowless grave, but a place
>   I may go both in and out of.[11]

This, of course, is "Bless what there is for being," the attitude of "Precious Five." But as well as being an acceptance, it is also a thanksgiving. The desire here is neither for a recovery of a lost Eden outside of time nor for an end to time through death, but for precisely what there is: a life in time where a man is able to say, with some conviction,

> . . . I ought
>   to outlast the limber dragonflies
>
> as the muscle-bound firs are certainly
>   going to outlast me, . . .

a life where there is freedom and movement in one's own "house," order in one's own domain.

[11] W. H. Auden, *About the House* (New York: Random House, 1965), p. 7.

From this introduction Auden proceeds to examine each room and the people with whom he would like to share it. There is a poem for each room, and all of them are light and affirmative in tone, intended to be no more than what they seem. Moreover, in each of them it is Auden as man, barely veiled by any mask and speaking more to himself than to others, who interests us rather than the ideas expounded.

The second half of *About the House* is, as its title "In and Out" implies, a potpourri of different poems on different themes. There are poems about places visited (Iceland, Norway, America); occasional poems ("A Toast: Christ Church Gaudy, 1962," "A Short Ode to a Philologist: J. R. R. Tolkien," "Elegy for JFK," and "Lines for Elizabeth Mayer"); four transliterations; and various other poems of varying lengths and subjects. Nonetheless, there is a unity to "In and Out" which is perhaps best seen in the first and last poems of the section.

The first, "A Change of Air," deals with man's urge to change his environment. Auden cautions against pursuing this impulse too seriously ("the flashy errands of your dreams"), for no matter where one goes the same self goes along, and, when one returns (as one always does), the same self also returns. The poem gives a light-verse version of the dangers of attempting to escape from one's self that were more seriously dealt with in *The Sea and the Mirror* and *The Age of Anxiety*. We are what we are and there is little we can do about it; the results of any journey to prove that significant change is possible will always add up to almost nothing.

The last poem in the volume, "Whitsunday in Kirchstetten," is one of the most direct and personal poems Auden has written, and it contains perhaps the most complete statement of Auden's feelings towards himself, his world, and his God. It is a quite literal recreation of a church service ("Herr Beer / picks up our

slim offerings and Pfarrer Lustkandl / quietly gets on
with the Sacrifice") at a time when any kind of faith
seems rather silly, for,

. . . Blake's Old Nobodaddy
. . . .
the Big White Christian upstairs, is dead,
and won't come hazing us no more, nor bless our bombs.

Yet faith there is, in spite of the fact that "The Holy
Ghost / does not abhor a golfer's jargon" and that
"ninety kilometers from here our habits end, / where
minefield and watchtower say NO EXIT." There is still
the individual commitment which comes (as is typical
of Auden at this stage) with the self-deprecating "I'm
just an ordinary man" attitude of the aging intellectual.
He says:

. . . There is no Queen's English
in any context for *Geist* or *Esprit:* about
catastrophe or how to behave in one
I know nothing, except what everybody knows—
if there when Grace dances, I should dance.

There stands Auden. The social or psychological
worries are over. About his house or about the world he
has the confidence of knowing that he knows nothing.
He has consciously tried to circumscribe his universe
until it contains only himself, his friends, and his God.
He has done it. The search seems to be over (of this, of
course, one can never be sure) and the final mask
assumed. The end of the search is no different, really,
from the end of "The Seven Stages" of *The Age of Anxiety;* only the attitude has changed. Where once the
sight of the world as it is brought horror or despair, it
now commands only an amused, accepting smile. It is
the stance of a man who has tried to understand both
himself and the world and has given up; he has, however, surrendered with grace and, Auden would add, to
Grace.

138

VI

"Grace Dances"

STEPHEN SPENDER has remarked that he feels the idea
which unites all of Auden's work (enclosing it "like the
sides of a box") is "Symptom and Cure." [1] The various
symptoms all stem from a need to love, and the various
cures are to be found in different types of love at different stages of Auden's career. To the extent that any
generalization about a poet's career can be true, Spender's feeling that "the direction of Auden's poetry has
been towards the defining of the concept of love" seems
to be accurate, and my purpose here has been to show
the effect this search for definition has had upon the
"voice" or the persona in his poetry.

"Petition," taken as an example of Auden's early
work, has at its center a belief in the redemption of the
world. The petitioner, the early Auden persona, believes that "Sir" need only serve as a guide to the way-
ward, and mankind will progress to "New styles of
architecture." Historical time is beneficent—man must
only make use of it. The persona of "Petition" is a doc-
tor/teacher urging man to heal himself and then his
society. He appears as a leader, proud, with his flock of
converts ever-growing behind him.

We have already seen, in Chapter I, how Auden became disillusioned during the thirties and began searching in new directions, influenced most notably by

1 "W. H. Auden and His Poetry," *Auden: A Collection of Critical
Essays*, ed. Monroe K. Spears, p. 28. Spender's remarks are quoted
at length in note 2 of Chapter I.

Charles Williams. The poetic results of these developments culminate in "September 1, 1939." History is there viewed as a great betrayer; as a consequence, the persona of "September 1, 1939" is no leader, for there is nowhere to lead people. Instead, he is alone, frightened, "Beleaguered by . . . / Negation and despair," and his only hope is that he may "Show an affirmative flame." Auden has lost his beliefs in the old cures, but he has not yet joined the coinherence. His persona embodies this; "he" is "In solitude," searching "for company." The voice is that of Auden's middle period. There is no surety in the poems of the late thirties and early forties because there is no surety in the man himself.

The search for a positive position (or, as Spender would term it, a new definition of "the concept of love") led Auden into the labyrinth of the long, dramatic poems of the forties. Although we know from his earlier work (particularly the collaboration with Isherwood) that Auden had (and for that matter still has) an interest in dramatic form, it seems to be more than "interest" that produces the complexity of *The Sea and the Mirror, For the Time Being,* and *The Age of Anxiety.* My guess is that Auden wrote these works, at least in part, to purge his old persona (the persona of "September 1, 1939" is, after all, really just the persona of "Petition" with his world gone bad) and to give himself time to find and develop a new one. This explanation might offer a reason why, for instance, in spite of the multiplicity of voices in the three long works, the voice of "In Praise of Limestone" comes as such a surprise when it says, "Dear, I know nothing."

The conflict in all three of the dramatic works lies in man's problems in adjusting to his world. All three works are Christian in that they are based on the belief in Christ's birth, death, and Godhood as fact. Yet, instead of singing the joys concomitant with this fact, they focus on the problems that the possibility of redemption has presented to man.

The Auden of "Petition" could offer praise to man's "becoming" in the worldly, social sense—to mankind's improvement within historical time. The Auden of "Horae Canonicae" is able to celebrate the mystery of redemption without rendering the world of the moment meaningless. But the Auden of *The Sea and the Mirror, For the Time Being,* and *The Age of Anxiety* seems restless; no longer able to believe in "becoming," he is not yet able to accept "the Time Being" for what it is (or for what he later comes to see it as): his particular moment in historical time transformed by the glimpse of meaning beyond it seen in the appearance of God in human form. Consequently in these works ignorance leads to dread. Caliban, for instance, seems secure and is able to bring everyone together and preach the word because he knows that the other world exists and is eager to tell us so. This is the typical "old" Auden—Caliban as his persona has found a cure and is passing it on. Yet, if we readjust Caliban slightly, place him within reality and confront him with the necessity of trying to do something with his knowledge, we end up in the predicament of Malin. Malin, at the conclusion of *The Age of Anxiety,* marks the death of the "old" Auden persona, the teacher-preacher-healer who dispenses a variety of remedies throughout most of Auden's poetry from "Petition" to *For the Time Being.* It has been noted before that Malin is a medical intelligence officer. This is of considerable significance because in this role he brings together all of Auden's secular heroes. He is an officer, therefore a leader; a medical officer, therefore a healer; a medical intelligence officer, therefore potentially a teacher (in fact, Auden tells us that he was). He has all the qualifications for the perfect secular hero; moreover, he even knows about Christ. But Malin is a failure. His journeys and rituals (his "cures") end in failure and seem more malicious than well-meant. There is nothing he can do to save "the Time Being" or to light the way towards a better future. He and his companions merely return to the endless futility of their daily lives.

The inability of Malin to transform or transcend his life through knowledge signals the end of Auden's interest in the ethical hero (the man who possesses knowledge others do not have), the enlightened secular leader who dominates Auden's poetry, in one variation or another, from his earliest works up to the exposure of Malin. Caliban still exhibits the compulsion to preach and proselytize, and even in the original version of "September 1, 1939" we can hear the voice admonish, "we must love one another or die."

The Age of Anxiety brings to an end the possibility of teaching and preaching mankind's reform. Auden's new belief is that truth can be conveyed to another only through personal *example,* and it indicates the dominant influence of Charles Williams on this phase of his development. According to Auden and Eliot, Williams demonstrated the existence of good by *being* good, not by questioning or analyzing good, and what Williams meant by good was believing in Christ as redeemer and in the doctrine of substitution as a way of life.

After finally rejecting the idea of a secular leader, Auden accepted this belief, and this acceptance effected a dramatic change in his poetry. Until the appearance of *Nones,* Auden's poetry had been characterized by a strong, direct "voice." This voice, whether positive as in the case of Caliban and the persona of "Petition," or negative as in the case of Malin, was the voice of a leader speaking from a position of authority and offering a program of reform. But Malin shows that knowledge by itself is useless, even dangerous. Moreover, the principle of equality inherent in the doctrine of substitution totally negates any idea of a leader-follower relationship.

Auden's emerging belief in the coinherence therefore made it necessary to find a new persona with an entirely different "voice." There were two alternatives. One, the religious hero, Auden immediately rejected as being impossible to portray in literature. In fact, his sole objection to Williams' novels was that Williams attempted to give them heroes. The alternative which Auden chose represented a complete break with his earlier work. Since the voice of the ethical hero was no longer meaningful and the voice of the religious hero impossible, Auden chose the voice of no hero at all—an ordinary, humble, aging man became his new persona. From *Nones* to *About the House*, he ambles through history and around the world, talking to us in a quiet, gentle voice about his own inadequacies and those of the world. He reminds us that Christ did, after all, die for us, but that it is up to us to discover the significance of this death for ourselves. As for himself, he says

> I know nothing, except what everyone knows—
> if there when Grace dances, I should dance.

The critical problem, of course, lies in passing a value judgment on Auden's "journey." There is a vast difference between Auden's poems of the thirties and his work of the forties and an almost equally vast difference between those poems and his later nondramatic work. One faces two temptations: that of merely dismissing the later poems as the product of a self-induced early senility, or, following Randall Jarrell's lead, that of getting mad at Auden and accusing him of lying to his readers. These temptations arise because it is very difficult in our increasingly cynical age to believe that Auden really takes his faith seriously. But if we admit right at the outset that he is *very* serious, we may examine the poems to see precisely what effect his change of beliefs had on them.

The power of Auden's early poetry (up to and including "September 1, 1939") came from the tension between the poet and his experience. Auden constantly reacted to his environment. He saw himself and his fellow men as being in conflict with their minds, each other, and the world around them. This conflict manifested itself in different ways but was always present. The ideology of the poems, though differing slightly as Auden passed through the influence of various dogmas, had as its basis a belief in the possibility of resolving the tension between man and his world. The poetry was propaganda poetry in perhaps the purest sense, offering only progress and the improvement, whatever it may be, of man and his world.

The persona of these early poems was an intense and interesting man. Central to his character was the need to know and, once he felt he had gained knowledge, the need to teach. The resultant effect of this "needing to" is a feeling of movement in the poems. We hear the voice of the persona admonishing us, as he moves from uncertainty to certainty and back to uncertainty, to look on ourselves and our world with hard, questioning eyes, accepting nothing as final, except death.

He says, "Follow me; but not without reservations. If I lead you down a blind alley I hope I will be the first to recognize it. But remember, it is your life and world as well as mine. I will not lie to you, but I may be wrong." He is a leader who respects his followers; a teacher who recognizes the possibility of error; a healer who realizes that there may well be more than one cure. There is no cynicism here. The persona of these poems, like the author, takes himself and his world very seriously. He may not know what is right, but he does know that knowledge exists and that it is man's responsibility to search for it.

If one were to give the above description of Auden's persona and verse to a prospective reader and then were to have him read the poems in *About the House* without telling him they were Auden's, his response would probably be, "What do these poems have to do with W. H. Auden?" The answer would be "Nothing," for although there are technical similarities between the work of the early Auden and that of the Auden of the sixties, the poems are written by what amounts to two different men and they show it; comparing them is like comparing the poems of Byron and Tennyson, or those of Pope and Blake.

The most important fact about the poetry of the "new" Auden, which one encounters for the first time in *Nones,* is the lack of tension between the poet and his experience. Both man and world simply are; no more, no less. The only problem, a nonmetaphysical one, is recognizing, accepting, and praising the existence of both. The "new" Auden seems to be telling us that all the agonies or hopes of the thirties were mere nonsense, just a kind of joke, the by-product of a frivolous and spent youth. Now that we have all grown up, we can, and should, realize that there simply is no such thing as progress and that the knowledge we were told to search for so diligently is valuable only as amusement; that poetry, like psychology or sociology, is silly business, mere froth and fun, an employment for idle hands and heads.

Experience no longer bothers Auden the poet; in fact, Auden the man no longer bothers Auden the poet. He has made a separate peace and now is able to turn and smile benignly at the rest of us. I think it is this smile that so irritated Jarrell, among others; no radical could stand to watch Lenin take off his coat and be revealed as an Anglican bishop. But what we think is smugness in the smile is only surety—Auden finally knows he is right; it is as simple as that. As a result, he no longer will permit our questions; we may either accept or reject his stand and his work, but we may no longer hope for "a change of heart."

A Selected Bibliography

THE BOOKS AND ARTICLES listed in the following bibliography are restricted to those which were most valuable to me. For more comprehensive lists of works by and about Auden during the period 1940–1966, the reader should consult the bibliographies of Barry Bloomfield, Edward Callan, and Joseph P. Clancy (listed below), and the footnotes and texts of John H. Blair's *The Poetic Art of W. H. Auden* and Monroe K. Spears' *The Poetry of W. H. Auden: The Disenchanted Island*.

Auden, W. H. *About the House*. New York, 1965.

———. *The Age of Anxiety*. New York, 1947.

———. *Another Time*. New York, 1940.

———. "Augustus to Augustine," *The New Republic*, September 25, 1944, pp. 373–376. A review of *Christianity and Classical Culture* by Charles N. Cochrane.

———. "Balaam and the Ass: The Master-Servant Relationship in Literature," *Thought*, XXXIX (Summer, 1954), 237–270.

———. "The Christian Tragic Hero," *The New York Times Book Review*, December 16, 1954, p. 1. A review of *Moby Dick* by Herman Melville.

———. *The Collected Poetry of W. H. Auden*. New York, 1945.

———, ed. *Criterion Book of Modern American Verse*. New York, 1956.

———. *The Dance of Death*. London, 1933.

———. *The Double Man*. New York, 1941.

———. *The Dyer's Hand*. New York, 1962.

———. *The Enchaféd Flood*. New York, 1950.

Auden, W. H. "Eros and Agape," *The Nation*, June 28, 1941, pp. 756–758. A review of *Love in the Western World* by Denis de Rougemont.

————. *For the Time Being*. New York, 1944.

————. "Holding the Mirror Up to History," *The New Yorker*, September 25, 1954, pp. 131–138. A review of *The Hedgehog and the Fox* by Isaiah Berlin.

————. *Homage to Clio*. New York, 1960.

————. Introduction to *The American Scene* by Henry James, ed. W. H. Auden. New York, 1946. Pp. iv–ix.

————. Introduction to *The Descent of the Dove* by Charles Williams. New York, 1956. Pp. v–xiii.

————. Introduction to *Slick but not Streamlined*, poems by John Betjeman, ed. W. H. Auden. New York, 1947. Pp. vi–xiii.

————. "The Ironic Hero: Some Reflections on Don Quixote," *Horizon*, XX (August 1949), 86–94.

————. "Jacob and the Angel," *The New Republic*, December 27, 1939, pp. 292–293. A review of *Behold This Dreamer* by Walter de la Mare.

————. "K's Quest," in *The Kafka Problem*, ed. Angel Flores. New York, 1946. Pp. 47–52.

————. "A Knight of the Infinite," *The New Republic*, August 21, 1944, pp. 223–224. A review of *Gerard Manley Hopkins: A Life* by Eleanor Ruggles.

————, ed. *The Living Thoughts of Kierkegaard*. New York, 1952.

————. *Look Stranger*. London, 1936.

————. "The Means of Grace," *The New Republic*, June 2, 1941, pp. 765–766. A review of *The Nature and Destiny of Man* by Reinhold Niebuhr.

————. "Nature, History and Poetry," *Thought*, XXV, 98 (September 1950), 415–430.

————, ed. *Nineteenth Century British Minor Poets*. New York, 1966.

————. *Nones*. New York, 1951.

————. *On This Island*. New York, 1937.

————. *The Orators*. London, 1932.

————. *Poems*. London, 1930.

————. *Poems*. New York, 1934.

——. "The Poet of the Encirclement," *The New Republic*, October 25, 1943, pp. 579–581. A review of *A Choice of Kipling's Verse*, ed. T. S. Eliot.

——, ed. *The Portable Greek Reader*. New York, 1948.

——. "A Preface to Kierkegaard," *The New Republic*, May 15, 1944, pp. 683–686. A review of *Either/Or* by Søren Kierkegaard, ed. and trans. Swenson and Lowrie.

——. *Selected Poetry*. New York, 1959.

——. *The Shield of Achilles*. New York, 1955.

——. *Spain*. London, 1937.

——. "Tract for the Times," *The Nation*, January 4, 1941, pp. 24–25. A review of *Christianity and Power Politics* by Reinhold Niebuhr.

——. "Tradition and Value," *The New Republic*, January 15, 1940, pp. 90–91. A review of *The Novel and the Modern World* by David Daitches.

——. Untitled essay in *Modern Canterbury Pilgrims*, ed. James A. Pike. New York, 1956. Pp. 32–43.

——, and John Garrett, eds. *The Poet's Tongue*. London, 1935.

——, and Christopher Isherwood. *The Ascent of F6*. New York, 1937.

—— ——. *The Dog Beneath the Skin*. New York, 1935.

—— ——. *Journey to a War*. London, 1939.

—— ——. *On the Frontier*. New York, 1938.

——, and Louis Kronenberger, eds. *The Viking Book of Aphorisms*. New York, 1962.

——, and Louis MacNeice. *Letters from Iceland*. New York, 1937.

——, and Normal Holmes Pearson, eds. *Poets of the English Language*. 5 vols. New York, 1950.

Bartlett, Phyllis, and John A. Pollard. [On "September 1, 1939."] *The Explicator*, XIV (November 1955), 8.

Bayley, John Oliver. *The Romantic Survival; A Study in Poetic Evolution*. London, 1960.

Beach, Joseph Warren. *The Making of the Auden Canon*. Minneapolis, 1957.

Blair, John G. *The Poetic Art of W. H. Auden*. Princeton, 1965.

Bloomfield, Barry Cambray. *W. H. Auden, A Bibliography: The Early Years Through 1955.* Charlottesville, 1964.

Brooks, Cleanth. *Modern Poetry and the Tradition.* Chapel Hill, 1939.

Brown, Abigail B. "The Benign Wizard: A Study in the Cosmology and Later Poetry of W. H. Auden." Unpublished Master's thesis, Columbia University, 1948.

Brown, Wallace Cable. [On "Petition."] *The Explicator,* III, 5 (March 1945), 38.

Callan, Edward. "Allegory in Auden's *The Age of Anxiety,*" *Twentieth Century Literature,* X (January 1965), 155–165.

――――. *An Annotated Checklist of the Works of W. H. Auden* (1924–1957). Denver, 1958.

――――. "Auden's 'New Year Letter': A New Style of Architecture," *Renascence,* XVI (1963), 13–19.

Clancy, Joseph P. "A W. H. Auden Bibliography 1924–1955," *Thought,* XXX (Summer, 1955), 260–270.

Cowley, Malcolm. "Virtue and Virtuosity: Notes on W. H. Auden," *Poetry,* LXV (January 1945), 202–209. A review of *For the Time Being.*

Dupee, F. W. "Verse Chronicle," *The Nation,* October 28, 1944, pp. 537–538. A review of *For the Time Being.*

Elton, William. "Metapoetry by a Thinking Type," *Poetry,* LXXI (November 1947), 90–94. A review of *The Age of Anxiety.*

"The Faith of W. H. Auden," anon. editorial, *The Christian Century,* January 16, 1946, pp. 71–73.

Freemantle, Ann. "Auden's Odyssey," *Commonweal,* May 25, 1945, pp. 141–143. A review of *The Collected Poetry.*

――――. "Wise Man's Sons," *Commonweal,* December 8, 1944, pp. 194–198. A review of *For the Time Being.*

Greenberg, Herbert Samuel. "Quest for the Necessary: A Study of the Poetry of W. H. Auden." Unpublished Ph.D. dissertation, University of Wisconsin, 1964.

Hartley, Anthony. "Empson and Auden," *Spectator,* December 9, 1955, pp. 815–816. A review of *The Shield of Achilles.*

Helland, Claire E. "An Analysis of W. H. Auden's *For the Time Being* and Its Relationship to Kierkegaardian Philosophy and the Medieval Mystery Plays." Unpublished Master's thesis, Columbia University, 1963.

Hoggart, Richard. *Auden; An Introductory Essay.* London, 1951.

Isherwood, Christopher. *Lions and Shadows.* Norfolk, Connecticut, 1947.

Jarrell, Randall. "Changes of Attitude and Rhetoric," *The Southern Review,* VII (1941), 326–349.

———. "Freud to Paul: The Stages of Auden's Ideology," *The Partisan Review,* XII (Fall, 1945), 437–457.

———. "Verse Chronicle," *The Nation,* October 18, 1947, pp. 424–425. A review of *The Age of Anxiety.*

Koch, Kenneth. "New Books by Marianne Moore and W. H. Auden," *Poetry,* XC (April 1957), 47–52.

Lechlitner, Ruth. "The Odyssey of Auden," *Poetry,* LXVI (July 1945), 204–215. A review of *The Collected Poetry.*

Levin, Harry. "Through the Looking Glass," *The New Republic,* September 18, 1944, pp. 347–348. A review of *For the Time Being.*

Lewars, Kenneth. "The Quest in Auden's Poems and Plays." Unpublished Master's thesis, Columbia University, 1947.

Lewis, C. Day. *The Buried Day.* New York, 1960.

Linebarger, James M. "W. H. Auden's *The Sea and the Mirror.*" Unpublished Master's thesis, Columbia University, 1957.

Mason, H. A. "Mr. Auden's Quartet," *Scrutiny,* XV (Spring, 1948), 155–160. A review of *The Age of Anxiety.*

New Verse. "Auden/Double Number." Nos. 26–27, (November 1937).

Olsen, Marilyn Jane. "A Study of *The Age of Anxiety* by W. H. Auden." Unpublished Master's thesis, Columbia University, 1959.

Replogle, Justin Maynard. "The Auden Group: The 1930's Poetry of W. H. Auden, C. Day Lewis, and Stephen Spender." Unpublished Ph.D. dissertation, University of Wisconsin, 1956.

———. "Auden's Intellectual Development 1950–1960," *Criticism,* VII (Summer, 1965), 250–262.

Robertson, D. A., Jr. [On "Petition."] *The Explicator,* III, 7 (May 1945), 51.

Sandeen, Ernest. "Facing the Muse," *Poetry*, XCVII (March 1961), 380–386. A review of *Homage to Clio*.

Scarfe, Francis. *Auden and After; The Liberation of Poetry*. London, 1942.

——. *W. H. Auden*. Monaco, 1945.

Smith, Hallett. [On "Petition."] *The Explicator*, III, 7 (May 1945), 51.

Southworth, J. G. *More American Poets*. London, 1954.

Spears, Monroe K., ed. *Auden: A Collection of Critical Essays*. Englewood Cliffs, New Jersey, 1964.

——. "The Dominant Symbols of Auden's Poetry," *The Sewanee Review*, LIX (July–September 1951), 392–425.

——. *The Poetry of W. H. Auden: The Disenchanted Island*. New York, 1963.

Spender, Stephen. *Poetry Since 1939*. London, 1946.

——. "Seriously Unserious," *Poetry*, LXXVIII, 6 (September 1951), 352–356. A review of *Nones*.

——. "W. H. Auden and His Poetry," in *Auden: A Collection of Critical Essays*, ed. Monroe K. Spears. Englewood Cliffs, New Jersey, 1964.

——. *World Within World*. London, 1951.

Sunesen, Bent. "All We Are Not Stares Back at What We Are," *English Studies*, XL (December 1958), 439–449.

Stauffer, Donald A. "Which Side Am I Supposed to Be On?," *Virginia Quarterly Review*, XXII (Autumn, 1946), 570–580.

Wilder, Amos N. *Modern Poetry and the Christian Tradition*. New York, 1952.

Wimsatt, W. K., Jr. [On "Petition."] *The Explicator*, III, 7 (May 1945), 51.